D11125779

About the author

Peter Rosset, PhD, is a food rights activist, agro-ecologist and rural development specialist. He is based in Chiapas, Mexico, where he is a researcher at the Centro de Estudios para el Cambio en el Campo Mexicano (Centre for Studies of Rural Change in Mexico), and coordinator of the Land Research Action Network (www.landaction.org). He is also Global Alternatives Associate of the Centre for the Study of the Americas and is a Visiting Scholar in the Department of Environmental Science, Policy and Management of the University of California, Berkeley. His previous books include: *The Case for a GM-Free Sustainable World* (2003), *Sustainable Agriculture and Resistance: Transforming Food Production in Cuba* (Food First Books, 2002) and *World Hunger: Twelve Myths* (Grove Press, 1998), among others.

Food is Different

*Why We Must Get the WTO
Out of Agriculture*

Peter M. Rosset

Fernwood Publishing
Halifax, Nova Scotia

Books for Change
Bangalore

SIRD
Kuala Lumpur

David Philip
Cape Town

Zed Books
London & New York

Food is Different: Why We Must Get the WTO Out of Agriculture was first published in 2006 by

In Canada: Fernwood Publishing,
32 Oceanvista Lane, Site 2A, Box 5,
Black Point, Nova Scotia, BOJ IBO

In India: Books *for* Change,
139 Richmond Road, Bangalore 560 025

In Malaysia: Strategic Information Research Development (SIRD),
No. 11/4E, Petaling Jaya, 46200 Selangor

In Southern Africa: David Philip (an imprint of New Africa Books),
99 Garfield Road, Claremont 7700, South Africa

In the rest of the world: Zed Books Ltd, 7 Cynthia Street, London NI 9JF, UK,
and Room 400, 175 Fifth Avenue, New York, NY 10010, USA
www.zedbooks.co.uk

Designed and typeset in Monotype Bembo by Long House, Cumbria, UK
Cover designed by Andrew Corbett

Distributed in the USA exclusively by Palgrave Macmillan, a division of
St Martin's Press, LLC, 175 Fifth Avenue, New York, NY 10010

A catalogue record for this book is available from the British Library
US CIP Data is available from the Library of Congress

Library and Archives Canada Cataloguing in Publication
Rosset, Peter
    Food is different : why we must get the WTO out of agriculture / Peter
M. Rosset.
Includes bibliographical references and index.
ISBN 1-55266-201-2
    1. Produce trade--Government policy. 2. World Trade Organization.
3. Agriculture and state. 4. Produce trade. 5. Agricultural systems. I. Title.

HF2651.F27R68 2006   382'.41   C2006-902031-0

ISBN 1 84277 754 8 Hb (Zed Books)
ISBN 1 84277 755 6 Pb (Zed Books)
ISBN 978 1 84277 754 1 Hb (Zed Books)
ISBN 978 1 84277 755 8 Pb (Zed Books)

Transferred to digital printing in 2007.

Contents

Tables, Figures and Boxes

Table

Figures

Boxes

Abbreviations

ACP	Africa, Caribbean and Pacific bloc
CAFTA	Central America Free Trade Agreement
CAP	Common Agricultural Policy
CCC	Commodity Credit Corporation
CIRAD	Agricultural Research Centre for International Development (France)
COOL	Country of Origin Labeling
CP	Conservation Percentage
CPE	European Farmers Coordination
CSP	Conservation Security Program
EAGGF	European Agricultural Guidance and Guarantee Fund
EQIP	Environmental Quality Incentives Program
ERS	Economic Research Service
EU	European Union
FAO	Food and Agriculture Organization (of the United Nations)
FFFA	Food from Family Farms Act
FOR	Farmer Owned Reserve
FSR	Food Security Reserve
FTAA	Free Trade Area of the Americas
GATS	General Agreement on Trade in Services
GATT	General Agreement on Tariffs and Trade
GE foods	genetically-engineered foods
GIPSA	Grain Inspection and Packers Stockyards Administration
GMOs	genetically-modified organisms
IATP	Institute for Agriculture and Trade Policy
ILO	International Labor Organization
IMF	International Monetary Fund
IPRs	Intellectual Property Rights
LDCs	Least-Developed Countries

LDP	Loan Deficiency Payment
NAFTA	North American Free Trade Agreement
NFFC	National Family Farm Coalition
QRs	Quantitative Restrictions
ROPPA	West African Network of Peasant and Agricultural Producers' Organizations
SAPs	structural adjustment programs
SCM	Subsidies and Countervailing Measures
SPs	special products
SSM	special safeguard mechanism
TBT	Technical Barriers to Trade
TNCs	transnational corporations
TRIPS	Trade-Related Aspects of Intellectual Property Rights
TRQ	tariff rate quota
UNCTAD	United Nations Conference on Trade and Development
US	United States
USDA	United States Department of Agriculture
WTO	World Trade Organization

This book is dedicated to Lee Kyung Hae, the peasant farm leader from South Korea, a member of the Via Campesina delegation, who courageously gave his life on 10 September 2003, in Cancún, Mexico, in the struggle against the World Trade Organization, and in favor of that better world which is possible.

Acknowledgments

I would like to thank the following people who gave me moral support, discussed the issues covered in this book with me, and/or commented on earlier drafts: María Elena Martínez, Nico Verhagen, Raj Patel, Ana de Ita, George Naylor, Mark Weisbrot, Michael Conroy, Paul Nicholson, Shalmali Guttal, Luis Hernandez Navarro, Jacques Berthelot, Silvia Ribeiro, Alberto Gomez, Fausto Torres, João Pedro Stédile, Sophia Murphy, Andrianna Natsoulas, Alberto Villareal, Jerry Maldonado, Nadia Roumani and many others. This book is partially based on an earlier working paper I wrote for the Global Policy Innovations Project of the Carnegie Council on Ethics and International Affairs. My work on that paper was supported by the Rockefeller Brothers Fund.

The inspiration for this book comes from Lee Kyung Hae and the other courageous peasant, indigenous, family farm, and landless rural workers of La Via Campesina, and their many member organizations, including the MST (Brazil), UNORCA (Mexico), the National Family Farm Coalition (USA), the European Farmers Coordination, the Korean Peasants League, the Korean Women Peasants Association, FSPI (Indonesia), ATC (Nicaragua), the National Farmers' Union (Canada), the Assembly of the Poor (Thailand) and UNAC (Mozambique), among many others, who lead the global struggle against the World Trade Organization (WTO) and free trade, and in favor of food sovereignty. It is also inspired by the Zapatistas of Mexico, who rose up with the cry of *Basta!* on 1 January 1994, the day the North American Free Trade Agreement (NAFTA) went into effect.

A Ballad for Lee Kyung Hae

From the song *Lee Kyung Hae* by Stephan Smith[1]

I'll tell you the story about Lee Kyung Hae
Who left us in Cancún on Chusok Day.
A farmer from South Korea he did come
And in a pit of vipers he saved ten lives with one.

From high up in Jangzu, where the rice fields meet the trees
On the mountain slopes where the paddies get covered with snow and freeze
From land that the bankers had said no fruit could bear
He brought in a harvest the likes none could compare.

'Til the fame of his farming had spread both far and wide
And the people came flocking to live and work by his side
To learn how the farmer could still support his home
While the value of rice was pushed to an all-time low.

But then a great flood of rice from overseas
Came in at a price four times as low and brought him to his knees.
Three million rice farmers in twelve years lost their land
And Lee Kyung Hae was among them with his head down in his hands.

In the year that he lost his farm so dear he also buried his bride
While farmers all through the country gave up in suicide.
With nothing left to lose Lee did choose to spend the rest of his days
To speak for the farmers who can no longer live from their pay.

And when the bankers who'd taken his farm were gathered on Chusok Day
Lee with his life that was already lost jumped up on the barricades
And there in a ritual suicide these last words he did say:
'It's better for one man to die to save ten than for ten to die every day.'

Prologue

Speak the Truth:
Exclude Agriculture from the WTO!

LEE KYUNG HAE

KOREAN ADVANCED FARMERS FEDERATION

This is Lee's own story, edited from a statement he distributed in Cancún, Mexico on 10 September 2003, before he climbed up on the barricades and took his own life with a knife plunged into his heart, during the farmer and peasant protests against the World Trade Organization (WTO).

I am 56 years old, a farmer from South Korea who strove to solve our problems with great hope in the organization of farmers' unions. But I have mostly failed, as many other farm leaders elsewhere have failed. *What shall I do?*

Soon after the Uruguay Round Agreement was sealed [and led to the WTO], we Korean farmers realized that our destinies are no longer in our own hands. We cannot seem to do anything to stop the waves that have destroyed our communities, where we have been settled for hundreds of years. To make myself brave, I have tried to find the real reason and the real force behind those waves. And I reached the conclusion, here in front of the WTO. I am crying out my words to you, that have for so long boiled in my body:

I ask: For whom do you negotiate now?
For the people, or for yourselves?
Stop basing your WTO negotiations on flawed logic and mere diplomatic gestures.
Take agriculture out of the WTO system.

Our fears became reality in the marketplace. We soon realized that despite our best efforts we could never match the prices of cheap imports. We had to be aware that our farm size (1.3 hectares on average) is a mere one-hundredth of the farms in the large exporting countries. It is true that Korean agricultural reform programmes increased the productivity of individual farms. However, it is also a fact that increased productivity simply added further volume to over-supplied markets in which imported goods occupied the lowest price portion. Since massive importing began we small farmers have never been paid as much as our production costs. Sometimes, prices would drop four times over, all of a sudden. *What would be your emotional reaction if your salary drops suddenly to a half without knowing clearly the reason?*

The farmers who gave up early went to urban slums. Others who have tried to escape from the vicious cycle have met with bankruptcy due to accumulated debts. For me, I couldn't do anything but just look around at the vacant houses in the village, old and decaying. Once I went to a house where a farmer took his life by drinking a toxic chemical because of his uncontrollable debts. I could do nothing but listen to the howling of his wife. *If you were me, how would you feel?*

Widely paved roads lead to large apartments, buildings, and factories in Korea. The lands being paved now were mostly rice paddies built by generations over thousands of years. They used to provide the daily food and materials. And the ecological and hydrological functions of paddies are even more crucial to society. *Who will protect our rural vitality, community traditions, amenities, and environment?*

I believe that the situation of farmers in many other countries is similar. We have in common the problems of dumping, import surges, lack of government budgets. Tariff protection would be the practical solution. I have been so worried watching TV and hearing the news that starvation is prevalent in many less developed countries, although the international price of grain is so cheap.

Earning money through trade should not be their means of securing food. *Farmers need access to land and water. Charity? No! Let them work again!*

My warning goes out to all citizens that human beings are in an endangered situation. That uncontrolled multinational corporations and a small number of big WTO members are leading an undesirable globalization that is inhumane, environmentally degrading, farmer-killing, and undemocratic. It should be stopped immediately. Otherwise the false logic of neoliberalism will wipe out the diversity of global agriculture and be disastrous to all human beings. *WTO Kills Farmers!*

Foreword
Farmers Around the World Lose Out Under the WTO

GEORGE NAYLOR

PRESIDENT OF THE NATIONAL FAMILY
FARM COALITION, USA

George Naylor grows corn and soybeans in Iowa. The National Family Farm Coalition (NFFC)[2] is a voice for grassroots farm groups on farm, food, trade and rural economic issues, to ensure fair prices for family farmers, safe and healthy food for consumers, and vibrant, environmentally sound rural communities in America and around the world. The NFFC (founded in 1986) represents family farm and rural groups in 30 states whose members face the challenge of the deepening economic recession in rural communities that is primarily caused by low farm prices and by the increasing corporate control of agriculture.

Despite claims of generous concessions, like 60 per cent cuts in domestic support, the only sure outcome of the American government's World Trade Organization (WTO) proposals is trade rules that continue to benefit multinational grain and livestock corporations with cheap commodities, by pitting farmers around the world against each other in expanded international markets. The US touts the benefits and professes the obligations of free trade, while at the same time scheming to continue subsidy programs to keep the US farm economy functioning in the face of disastrously low commodity prices for farmers.

After all, the subsidies are a product of fashioning US farm bills to meet the criteria of 'free markets' – the elimination of price floors, border controls, food security reserves, and conservation set-asides. With the inherent uncertainty of commodity markets, and the tendency of prices to decline in real dollars over time, the US farm system would collapse without a subsidy scheme to diminish uncertainty and provide liquidity to the farm economy. Bankers wouldn't loan farmers the money to plant the next crop without subsidies, given the extremely low prices of commodities and the possibility that they may go lower. Naturally, many developing countries can't offer even a modicum of government payments to avoid an agricultural train wreck. The combination of demanding market access, and refusing to restore supply management measures to raise agricultural prices, is a recipe for global rural hardship. Liberalizing of trade though the WTO or other free trade agreements – *with or without US subsidies* – will further destroy every country's food sovereignty and hasten the exodus of rural people from their beloved communities.

The obfuscation surrounding US proposals is nothing new to observers of years of agribusiness lobbying and victories resulting in 'market-oriented' farm programme legislation. The American people would not have chosen the type of agriculture we have – diminishing numbers of family farms being replaced by large, chemical-intensive crop farms and polluting, factory-farm livestock operations.

By playing games with the Amber, Blue and other coloured 'boxes' of the WTO negotiations,[3] the US continually circumvents member-country criticisms and various WTO rulings to the effect that many types of US subsidy payments violate WTO limits on domestic support. One prime example is the attempt to place counter-cyclical payments in the exempt Blue box, even though these payments have nothing to do with limiting production, the function supposedly assigned to Blue box measures. The US government, in representing the interests of multinational agribusiness, kills two birds with one stone – by making the counter-cyclical payments exempt from cuts, and by expunging any reference to supply management which is anathema to the interests and ideology of these giant corporations.

For the final insult, US farmers take the rap as being 'subsidized', while it is actually the corporations buying the cheap commodities that reap the benefits of the US subsidy scheme and of further trade liberalization. Farmer incomes, even with government payments, are a fraction of what they would be under previous, now defunct programmes that more nearly aimed at paying farmers at least our cost of production and required the buyers to pay that price, rather than the American taxpayers.

For instance, look at the most widely produced crop in the United States, corn (maize), that is grown on nearly 80 million acres (32 million hectares) and is used mostly for livestock feed, domestically or overseas. The national average price for corn in 1978 was $2.25 per bushel (1 bushel = 56 pounds or 25.5 kilos), recovering from $1.50 in the fall of 1977, because the Secretary of Agriculture had raised the support price to $2 and implemented a land set-aside programme. This was still well below the lofty prices of over $3 in the early 1970s. If one were to adjust the $2.25 price for inflation since 1978 – 300 per cent – corn today would go for $6.75 per bushel. Instead, the 2005 price of corn in the western corn belt was $1.35, and sometimes less. The farmer has to produce four times as many bushels to buy something today as back in 1978. Even with loan deficiency payments, direct payments, and counter-cyclical payments, the resulting equivalent price is approximately $2.25 per bushel in 2005 dollars – one-third of the 1978 price in real dollars! USDA calculations of cost of production, yields, and prices for 2003 and 2004 show an economic loss for corn farmers in virtually every region of the country without government payments.[4] It is only direct and counter-cyclical payments that allow these farmers to break even or make any profit at all.

The $1.35 price (like similarly low prices for other commodities) radiates around the world, with the Chicago Board of Trade setting the benchmark price for every point on the planet. Dumping cheap

corn (and other commodities) is the order of the day.[5] Farmers in
other countries, already victims of tariff cuts from the International
Monetary Fund (IMF) and World Bank edicts, are further doomed
by the US proposals for 'market access'. They will find the only difference in their price from Chicago to be shipping and handling.
Multinational corporations like Cargill, Tyson, and Smithfield, that
have already destroyed diversified family farming in America by
feeding livestock cheap corn and soybean meal in giant polluting
feedlots, are further expanding this industrial model to other
countries every year. Legitimate uses of government support in
poor countries – for extension, agrarian reform, or balancing
regional inequities – are destined to failure when cheap commodity
prices drive farm incomes lower and lower.

Not only is the plague of cheap commodity and livestock prices
globally contagious, but so is the hypocritical US subsidy solution.
According to a recent article in *The Western Producer*, Canadian corn
producers recently received a preliminary ruling from the Canadian
Trade Tribunal that 'there is enough evidence of subsidy, dumping
and damage to continue the investigation' that might lead to duties
on US corn imports. This would lead to higher grain prices in
Canada, which corporate corn buyers do not like at all. The article
quotes Clare Schlegel, president of the Canadian Pork Council,
'We are absolutely opposed to the idea that an import duty solves
anything. We recognize that corn producers are suffering and we
want to walk along beside them in finding a solution that does not
involve raising our costs.' The agribusiness idea, of course, is to get
the Canadian government to make payments to corn producers to
keep them from going broke. That's the hypocritical solution *du
jour* for developed countries, making sure the payments are con-
veniently labeled Green box or Blue box, but it is an impossible
solution for poor developing countries.

How much evidence do the nations of the world need that
liberalizing trade – the goal of the WTO – is unworkable and
threatens the livelihoods of millions of farmers, the food security of

the world's population, and the functioning of our natural environment? Liberalizing trade in agriculture forces farmers to desperately
increase production, driving down prices, to get bigger by plunging
into debt, or to leave farming all together. Liberalizing trade in agriculture means we have no food security reserves: every bushel must
be dumped on the international market every year, regardless of
how low prices go, ensuring a stark misallocation of resources and a
wasteful use of these precious commodities. In an era of dramatic
climate change and international hostilities and terrorism, the folly
of liberalizing agricultural trade is even more apparent. The WTO
needs to get out of agriculture, period.

waste

   The United States government, which is supposed to be a
'government of the people, for the people, and by the people',
needs to stop its hypocritical pushing of trade liberalization, and
rather join millions of family farmers and peasants in the rebirth of
democracy through the principle of People's Food Sovereignty.
Food Sovereignty respects the right of every country and region to
establish food and farm policies based on their own needs and traditions, for food security, for conservation of natural resources, for the
fair distribution of economic opportunities, and for the right of
farmers to serve their local markets at a fair price.

whose
principle ?

   The US should take the lead in creating agricultural policy that
supports sustainable family farms and a healthy environment for
future generations, by passing a new 2007 Farm Bill respecting the
principles of food sovereignty. The National Family Farm
Coalition (USA) supports passage of the *Food from Family Farms
Act*,[6] which will: (1) create a fair price floor so that corporate buyers
pay for commodities, rather than taxpayers; (2) help create food
reserves so that bountiful crops create food security rather than
depressing prices; and (3) support conservation measures to prevent
wasteful overproduction and the destruction of our environment.

why do
we think
that they
would do
this?

   Rather than more liberalization of agricultural trade, the US
must take the lead in applying these basic mechanisms to the only
possible solution to the global farm and rural economic depression

[handwritten margin note, top left: how can we assume this will take a diff path then current ones?]

[handwritten margin note, top right: ⊗ WTO would argue that that's what they are doing]

and environmental degradation: international trade cooperation for international supply management, to put a stop to global over-production and farm prices that fall lower every year (even as consumers pay more and more, thanks to agribusiness concentration). According to Cargill, 90 per cent of food grown in the world does not cross national borders, yet just a handful of countries produce 90 per cent of the commodities in international commerce, and an even smaller number of multinational corporations, like Cargill, do almost all of the actual trading. It is these companies that are the only winners when farmers get paid prices of misery, as they use this dirt-cheap supply to capture the local markets of other countries, and of other farmers.

Furthermore, exporting at less than the cost of production creates a drag on national income. Pitting nations and their farmers against each other will lead to irreversible and unfathomable problems for future generations.

Claiming that the Doha Round of the WTO is a 'development round' is a mockery. Now is the time to say 'No!' to WTO and to the free trade ideology of multinational corporations. Now is the time for the people of the world to join hands to share in the responsibility of creating food security reserves and conservation programs to restore rural prosperity, and to prevent the destruction of the land, whether in the corn belt of the United States, the picturesque landscapes of Europe, the rice paddies of Asia, the pampas of Argentina, or the rain forest of Brazil.

[handwritten margin note, lower left: ⊗ how do we join hands to separate?]

Introduction

Trade versus Development?

Behind the extremely technical debate within the WTO, what is at stake above all are models of agricultural development. (Dr Bruno Losch, Agricultural Research Centre for International Development, France, 2004)[7]

In the Prologue to this book, we read the words of Lee Kyung Hae. Lee was a farmer leader from South Korea who made the supreme sacrifice by giving his life in protest against the World Trade Organization (WTO). On 10 September 2003, he climbed up on the police barricades surrounding the site of the Fifth Ministerial negotiations of the WTO, in Cancún, Mexico, with a sign bearing the now famous slogan: 'WTO Kills Farmers'. He then immolated himself with a knife to the heart, leaving the words that open this book as his legacy. Lee wasn't just anybody. He had founded a cooperative and a farmers' association in Korea, had been a state legislator, and had been recognized by the government of Korea and by the United Nations as an outstanding farmer. Yet he lost his land, as did millions of other Korean farmers, after his government signed the General Agreement on Tariffs and Trade (GATT) in 1992, which later became the WTO. This trade liberalization agreement opened the Korean market to a flood of very cheaply priced food imports, which cut the bottom out of the market for

Korean farmers.[8] Their income plunged, and many committed
suicide when they realized that, because crop prices couldn't cover
the payments on their crop loans, they would be the first in their
family history to lose the farm inherited from their ancestors to
bankruptcy. They could not live with that shame.

Korea is not the only country to be faced with an epidemic of
farmer suicides. The US and India, among others, are seeing a
similar phenomenon, for much the same reasons. Lee felt he had
failed as a farmer leader, failed to solve the problems facing his
constituency. In seeking the causes of the agricultural malaise
afflicting South Korea, he found that an undemocratic and non-
transparent institution based half-way around the world, in Geneva,
was the instrument of their pain. He felt he had to find a way to
transcend national borders in his protest against the WTO, to take
his struggle to the international stage. He found the way to do that
in Cancún, and I have dedicated this book to his courage and to
explaining why he and millions of farmers around the world are so
opposed to free trade treaties like the WTO.

Trade, globalization and development in the nations of the south[9]

Trade is the most important issue that defines the start of the
millennium. Since the 1970s the global economy has been
transformed by advances in communications and transport technology, making it possible for companies to shift production rapidly
around the world in search of lower wages and new markets.
Transnational corporations have used their financial and political
muscle to usher in an intense period of trade liberalization, in search
of the Holy Grail of free trade. Beginning with the Uruguay Round
of negotiations for the General Agreement on Tariffs and Trade
(GATT), one trade agreement or treaty after another has come up.
From the North American Free Trade Agreement (NAFTA) to the
WTO, the framework for free trade is being set in international law.

In general terms, we are moving from smaller, national economies, to larger regional or global economies. Whenever a larger economy is created, new economies of scale come into play. Large transnational companies using automated mass production technology to produce goods at low unit costs flood local markets at prices with which smaller, national companies using labour-intensive production practices cannot compete. As witnessed in Mexico under NAFTA, these smaller companies go out of business and hundreds of thousands of people are laid off as new high-tech factories hire far fewer workers. One result is fewer jobs are needed to manufacture the same quantity of goods. Another result is that profits shift from nationally-owned companies, which tend to reinvest locally, to transnational corporations (TNCs) based in distant nations, who rarely reinvest in the 'affected' country. Those who benefit are corporate stockholders in Northern countries.

It is not just factory workers who have found their employment prospects threatened. The practice of 'out-sourcing', by which companies use suppliers around the globe, pits everyone from workers on the line to computer programmers, chip designers, and automobile engineers in a global competition for jobs. The basis of that competition is who will work for less, accept part-time employment without benefits, and accept unsafe working conditions and toxic emissions in their backyard. It is a veritable race to the bottom.

In a short period of time we have seen the post-war period, which saw living standards around the world rise in tandem with productivity, give way to a new pattern in which productivity continues to rise but living standards begin to drop. The first region to face the new free trade policies was Latin America, through the so-called structural adjustment programs (SAPs) of the 1980s – now known as the 'lost decade' of Latin American economic development. Living standards of the poor majorities slipped back to pre-1960s levels. Next up were East and South-East Asia, where forced trade liberalization went hand in hand with the removal of currency controls. The result was the Asian financial crisis, and the collapse of some of the Third World's strongest economies. Now on the free trade agenda is Africa, with some of the economies least able to compete in the global economy.

As weaker economies are merged with stronger ones, a highly uneven playing field is created. The nature of most new trade agreements (as well as conditions imposed through World Bank and International Monetary Fund loans) is to require that national governments give up sovereignty over their domestic economies. These changes in national and global governance mechanisms have in their sum eroded the ability of governments in Southern nations to manage national development trajectories with a view to the broad-based human security of their citizens. Critically, their ability has been weakened to ensure the social welfare of poor and vulnerable people, achieve social justice, guarantee human rights, and protect and sustainably manage their natural resources.

In order to make way for increased import/export activity and export-promoting foreign investment, SAPs, regional and bilateral trade agreements, and GATT and World Trade Organization negotiations, have all shifted the balance of governance over national economies away from governments and toward market mechanisms and global regulatory bodies like the WTO. Southern governments have progressively lost the majority of the macro-economic policy tools used in the past to direct national economic development. They have been forced to cut government invest-ment drastically through deficit-slashing requirements, to unify exchange rates, to devalue and then float currencies, to virtually eliminate import quotas, tariff and non-tariff import barriers, to privatize state banks and other enterprises, and to slash or eliminate subsidies of all kinds, including social services and price supports for small farmers. In most cases, either in preparation for entering trade agreements, or with international financial institution (IFI) funding and/or guidance, governance over land tenure arrangements has followed suit, with privatization, land markets and market mechanisms coming to the fore, in search of greater investment in agricultural sectors.

While such changes have in some cases created new opportunities for poor people to exploit new niche markets in the global economy (organic coffee, for example), they have for the most part undercut both government-provided social safety nets and guarantees, and traditional community management of resources and cooperation in the face of crises. The majority of the poor still live in rural areas, and these changes have driven many of them to new depths of crisis in their struggle to sustain their livelihoods. Increasingly they have been plunged into an environment dominated by global economic forces, where the terms of participation have been set to meet the interests of the most powerful. Small farmers find the prices of the staple foods they produce dropping below the cost of production, in the face of cheap imports freed from tariffs and quotas. They are increasingly without the subsidized credit, marketing and prices which once helped support them, and their communal land tenure arrangements are under attack from legal reforms and private sector investors.

Around the world, the poorest of the poor are the landless in rural areas, followed closely by land-poor farmers, those whose poor-quality plots are too small to support a family. They make up the majority of the rural poor and hungry, and it is in rural areas that the worst poverty and hunger are found. The expansion of agricultural production for export, controlled by wealthy elites who own the best lands, continually displaces the poor to ever more marginal areas for farming. They are forced to fell forests located on poor soils, to farm thin, easily eroded soils on steep slopes, and to try to eke out a living on desert margins and in rainforests. As they fall deeper into poverty, and despite their comparatively good soil management practices, they are often accused of contributing to environmental degradation.

But the situation is often worse on the more favorable lands. The better soils are concentrated into large holdings dedicated to monocultural production for export through the intensive use of mechanization, pesticides, and chemical fertilizers. Many of our planet's best soils – which had earlier been sustainably managed for millennia by pre-colonial traditional agriculturalists – are today being rapidly degraded, and in some cases abandoned completely, in the short-term pursuit of export profits and competition. The productive capacity of these soils is rapidly being depleted by to soil compaction, erosion, waterlogging, and fertility loss, together with growing resistance of pests to pesticides and the loss of biodiversity.

The products harvested from these more fertile lands flow over-whelmingly toward consumers in wealthy countries. Impoverished local majorities cannot afford to buy all that is grown, and because they are not a significant market, national elites essentially see local people as a labor source – a cost of production to be minimized by keeping wages down and busting unions. The overall result is a downward spiral of land degradation and deepening poverty in rural areas. Even urban problems have rural origins, as the poor must abandon the countryside in massive numbers, migrating to cities where only a lucky few make a living wage, while the majority languish in slums and shanty towns.

If present trends toward free trade and accompanying land concentration and the accompanying industrialization of agriculture continue unabated, it will be impossible to achieve social or ecological sustainability. On the other hand, research shows the potential that could be achieved by local production and land redistribution. Small farmers are more productive, more efficient, and contribute more to broad-based regional development than do the larger corporate farmers who hold the best land and who benefit from free trade. Small farmers with secure tenure can also be much better stewards of natural resources, protecting the long-term productivity of their soils and conserving functional biodiversity on and around their farms. What we require is the political will to make different policy decisions. The crisis described in this book is not a product of Nature; rather, it is a human product made by policies such as those on trade, privatization and structural adjustment – and it can be unmade by different policies.

Only by changing our development trajectory from the model of free trade, mega-large farms, land concentration and displacement of peoples can we stop the downward spiral of poverty, low wages, rural–urban migration and environmental degradation. The combination of trade policies that protect domestic markets for staple crops with the reversal of national policy biases that artificially favour wealthy producers over small farmers and cities over rural areas, plus truly redistributive land reform, offers the possibility of a new development model with the potential to feed the poor, lead to broad-based economic development, and conserve biodiversity and productive resources. This alternative framework (similar to what La Via Campesina calls 'Food Sovereignty', discussed later in this book) would apply the lessons learned in the 'bottom-up' development models followed in the immediate post-war period by some of today's most successful economies – China, Japan, South Korea, Taiwan – where family farmers, made economically successful through policy decisions, formed the internal markets that were the backbone of economic development. Those countries followed policies that were virtually the exact opposite, the mirror-image, of the WTO-type free trade, 'trickle down' policies of today. In the last chapter of this book we examine alternative polices for agriculture, and for trade in food and other farm products, polices that could help us switch tracks toward the more sustainable model. But first we take a closer look at food, the essential ingredient for life itself provided by the farmers of the world, like Lee Kyung Hae.

What is food?

What is food? What is farming? Is food like any other commodity, like steel, or a microchip, or a pair of running shoes? Where a shoe made in a Nike factory in Indonesia is indistinguishable from a shoe made in a Nike factory in El Salvador? Where South Korean steel, made to the same specifications, is identical to US steel? Or is there something more to food, and to how it is produced?

Consider a refrigerated tomato, grown on a large mechanized plantation on land that once belonged to now-displaced peasant or indigenous farmers, picked while green and gassed to ripen, packed in plastic and Styrofoam, shipped from the Southern hemisphere because it's winter in the North, spending more money on fuel than the tomato itself is worth. Is this tomato the same as an in-season, vine-ripened, heirloom variety tomato grown by a local family farmer?

When we buy the former tomato in a supermarket, we support transnational corporations that make fertilizer, pesticides, hybrid or genetically modified seeds, tractors, mechanical harvesters, irrigation equipment and spray rigs, and others that run international shipping, and still others that own port and distribution networks, supermarket chains and advertising companies. Is buying this imported tomato in the supermarket the same as buying a tomato in a farmers' market, whether we are American or European or Japanese and buy from a local farm family, or Mexican, South Korean or Nigerian, and buy from a local peasant family, who produce the tomato with less or no chemicals and machines? Does our act of purchasing have the same impact on the world at large? On farm families? On the environment?

Now say we are a consumer in Mexico, and we eat tortillas made from maize three times a day. We could eat a tortilla made from maize grown by a peasant or indigenous family, enabling them to stay in the countryside with the income from selling maize. Maize of a flavorful and nutritious local variety, grown on their ancestral land, using millennia-old farming techniques that rely on little or no pesticides, and that conserve trees and a mosaic of cultivated and forested land in the local landscape. Or we could eat a tortilla made from cheap maize imported from the US, of a genetically engineered variety usually sold for animal feed rather than human consumption – maize for which an American farm family was paid so little that, despite eroding and exhausting their land with desperate overproduction to make ends meet, cutting down all trees and generating a new dust bowl, they are one bad harvest or price swing away from losing the farm. . . .

Food *is* different. It is not just any merchandise or commodity. Food means farming, and farming means rural livelihoods, traditions and cultures, and it means preserving, or destroying, rural landscapes. Farming means rural society, agrarian histories; in many cases, rural areas are the repositories of the cultural legacies of nations and peoples. Food can give us pleasure, it can taste good or bad, it can be good for us or it can be bad for us.

But if food is different, should it treated as any other merchandise in our global economy, traded at will across international borders, shipped around the world by boat, train, truck or plane, managed by faceless corporations that buy it as if it were all homogeneous and all the same? These are corporations who pit farmers against farmers in a terrible competition where the 'winners' are those who sell for less (perhaps because they get a subsidy payment to compensate them, or perhaps not), and who in selling for less destroy the local environment, give us an unhealthy product, and pave the way for their own bankruptcy and exit from agriculture, eventually swelling the ranks of the urban un- or under-employed. But who are given no chance to exit from that competition with their dignity, and livelihoods, intact. When farmers grow food for their own people, when they produce for local and national markets, they have a chance to escape that downward spiral. But when the staple foods that people eat are imported, and when local farmers must try to compete with cheap exports in the global economy, there is no chance.

What we are really talking about is development: rural development, local economic development, regional development, and national economic development. One path contributes to broad-based and inclusive local economic development, in which farmers earn money which they in turn spend at the shops of local townsfolk. The other path leads to social and economic devastation.

In opening a country's market to cheap imports, free trade sets a process in motion. First, a sudden drop in farm prices can drive already poor, indebted farmers off the land over the short term. Second, a more subtle effect kicks in. As crop prices stay low over the medium term, profits per unit area – per acre or hectare – stay low as well. That means the minimum area needed to support a family rises, contributing to abandonment of farm land by smaller, poorer farmers – land which then winds up in the hands of the larger, better-off corporate farmers who can compete in a low price environment by virtue of having so many hectares. They overcome the low-profit-per-hectare trap precisely by owning vast areas which add up to some profits overall (perhaps supplemented by taxpayer subsidies), even if they represent very little on a per hectare basis. The end result of both mechanisms is the further concentration of farm land within in the ever-fewer largest farms, which in turn has terrible consequences.[10]

In the United States, the question was asked more than half a century ago: what does the growth of large-scale, industrial agriculture – crops and livestock for long-distance shipping and export – mean for rural towns and communities? Walter Goldschmidt's classic 1940s study of California's San Joaquin Valley compared areas dominated by large corporate farms with those still characterized by smaller, family farms.[11]

In farming communities dominated by large corporate farms, nearby towns died off. Mechanization meant that fewer local people were employed, and absentee ownership meant that farm families themselves were no longer to be found. In these corporate-farm towns, the income earned in agriculture was drained off into larger cities to support distant enterprises, while in towns surrounded by family farms the income circulated among local business establishments, generating jobs and community prosperity. Where family farms predominated, there were more local businesses, paved streets and sidewalks, more schools, parks, churches, clubs, and newspapers, better services, higher employment, and more civic participation. Studies conducted since Goldschmidt's original work confirm that his findings remain true today.[12]

When we turn to the Third World we find a similar situation. On the one hand there is the devastation caused by free trade, land concentration and industrial export agriculture, while on the other we find local benefits derived from a small-farm, peasant economy. A recent study in Brazil shows how local towns and villages benefit from the commerce that is generated when estates belonging to absentee landlords are occupied by landless peasants from the Landless Workers' Movement (MST) and turned into productive family and cooperative peasant farming enterprises.[13] In one such municipality, Julho de Castilhos, the members of the MST settlement, who only possess 0.7 per cent of the land, actually pay 5 per cent of the taxes, making the settlement into the municipality's second largest rural tax payer.[14] In fact, studies from around the world show that smaller farms, that produce for local and national markets, are more productive and efficient, generate more employment, contribute more to social welfare and economic development, and take better care of the environment than do the larger, industrialized export estates that take advantage of freer trade to drive smaller farmers off their land.[15]

That is precisely why the world's family farm, peasant, farm worker and indigenous peoples' movements, organized in the international alliance called La Via Campesina, are against the global free trade in food and other agricultural products being negotiated in WTO and other free trade agreements. That is why they want to get the WTO out of food and agriculture.[16]

A global controversy

Recent world history has been marked by a global controversy over trade agreements and so-called 'free trade'. Within this larger controversy, issues of agricultural trade and farm subsidies have played a central role. At stake are not just relatively narrow measures like trade volumes, economic growth rates and farm productivity, but also the very future of our global food system, of each country's unique agriculture and farming systems, and of the livelihoods of rural peoples worldwide.

Food and agriculture have proved to be the most significant stumbling blocks along the way to re-structuring the global trading system. While opinions differ widely as to whether this is a bad or a good thing, there can be no doubt that disagreements about agricultural trade and subsidies, during the period leading up to and in Seattle during the 1999 Third Ministerial of the WTO, played a key role in the spectacular collapse of that meeting.

With disagreements between the US and the EU over each other's farm subsidies, and protectionism against each other's exports – including Europe's rejection of genetically engineered (GE) grain from the US – disagreements between Northern and Southern nations over market access and dumping in farm and food products, North–South disagreements over related issues like intellectual property rights (IPRs), the lack of transparency and democracy in the negotiations themselves, and the riots in the streets, Seattle placed trade issues squarely in the public eye.

Following Seattle, no significant progress on agriculture and related issues was made in 2001 at the Fourth WTO Ministerial in Doha, Qatar, nor in 2002 in Quito, Ecuador, where the same basic group of agriculture issues, accompanied by massive street protests by organizations of farmers and indigenous people, blocked significant advances in negotiations toward the Free Trade Area of the Americas (FTAA). After failing to reach agreement with Latin American trade ministers in Quito, then US Trade Representative Robert Zoellick said that if the US couldn't get what it wanted from the FTAA negotiations, it would get it in the WTO. Yet the next WTO Ministerial, held in Cancún, Mexico in September 2003, collapsed just as Seattle had, again stumbling over agriculture and again marked by massive street protests and the self-immolation of Lee Kyung Hae. Once again Zoellick responded in disgust:

> the key division at Cancún was between the *can*-do and the *won't*-do [countries]. For over two years, the US has pushed to open markets globally, in our hemisphere, and with sub-regions or individual countries. As WTO members ponder the future, the US will not wait: we will move towards free trade with *can*-do countries.

[handwritten margin note: even though US isn't practicing free trade]

True to his word, the US has increasingly used its muscle to negotiate bilateral and regional (like the CAFTA agreement with Central America) trade agreements in lieu of progress in the WTO or the FTAA.

Following up on Cancún, more massive street protests by farmers from Korea and around the world, at the 2005 Ministerial in Hong Kong – and basically the same disagreements among countries – led to a weak agreement, basically only agreeing to keep negotiating. Cancún and Hong Kong also marked the emergence of new Southern-country negotiating blocs, most famously the G20 group of countries with large agro-export potential, led by Brazil and India, and the G33, G90 and G120 blocs of less powerful Third World nations, each with its own agenda running counter to US and EU proposals.[17]

This book

The global debate over farm trade and subsidies is critical yet confusing, full of common misconceptions and government doublespeak. The goal of this book is to sort out this confusion, and to take a look at some possible alternative, commonsense policies that might offer a way out of the conundrum.

I first take a quick look at trade negotiations and trade liberaliza-tion, placing them in historical context, and reviewing some of the most familiar recent events, like the spectacular collapse of WTO meetings in 1999 in Seattle and Cancún in 2003, and the hard-fought stand-off in Hong Kong. I look at the key issues behind the controversy: what are the points of difference, and who is for what and who is against what. I then use the recent debate over cotton subsidies to open a discussion of some common misconceptions over issues like subsidies and dumping.

This is followed by a closer look at some examples – like Mexico, widely seen as the 'laboratory' in which to study the impact of trade agreements, because it falls within the North American Free Trade Area, and Africa, which is the 'new frontier' for the next generation of trade agreements.

Finally we take a look at a series of alternative policies for food and agriculture. For the purposes of proposing those alternatives, and presenting a critique of prevalent policy prescriptions, we must share common goals that can be used as criteria. For this purpose, I postulate that most people, in most countries, would agree that we want a food and agriculture system that:

- Provides every one of us with adequate, affordable, healthy, tasty and culturally appropriate food.

- Offers rural peoples in each of our countries the opportunity for a life with dignity, in which they earn a living wage for their labor and have the opportunity to remain in rural areas if they prefer not to migrate to cities.

- Contributes to broad-based, inclusive economic development at the local, regional and national level.

- Conserves rural environments and landscapes, and rural-based cultural and culinary traditions, based on the sustainable long-term management of productive natural resources (soils, water, genetic resources and other biodiversity) by rural peoples themselves.

While these goals constitute a yardstick shared by major global public constituencies, like family farm and consumer groups, environmentalists, food and agriculture unions, and others, they are less readily recognized by governments and the food and agriculture industries. Despite their widely publicized disagreements, which we examine here, most governments still currently embrace one form or another of market fundamentalist positions on food and agriculture, while public opinion worldwide decries what is happening to our food system and our rural areas as market principles are more widely applied. The solution for many is to take food and agriculture out of the narrow confines of 'trade issues', making them rather into issues of 'development', and even 'sovereignty', particularly what farmer organizations refer to as 'food sovereignty'. As pie-in-the-sky as that may sound, we present concrete, feasible policy proposals concerning dumping, supply management, anti-trust measures, subsidies, and venues for negotiations that could achieve just that.

I

Trade Negotiations
and Trade Liberalization

World trade negotiations geared toward agreements and treaties for 'trade liberalization' have been taking place continually since 1986, with the inauguration of the Uruguay Round of negotiations in the framework of the General Agreement on Tariffs and Trade (GATT), which became the World Trade Organization in 1995. Since the founding of the WTO the negotiations have been highlighted by a series of 'Ministerial meetings' where major decisions are supposed to be made by the highest level of government officials (especially trade and/or finance ministers). These meetings have been failures – on their own terms – almost as often as they have been successful. Differences over the regulation of agricultural trade and farm subsidies played central roles in the most publicized of the failures, in Seattle in 1999 and in Cancún, Mexico, in 2003. On the other hand, in 2004 a partial agreement on some agricultural issues paved the way for an agreement at the 2005 Hong Kong Ministerial to continue negotiating, on the basis of damaging concessions by Third World countries and weak promises by the United States and Europe. This essentially saved the WTO from outright collapse, allowing stalled negotiations to restart.[18]

Trade liberalization is the process of removing barriers to trade. The idea is to liberate trade and thus market forces from the taxes and regulations that hinder them – and government subsidies that distort them – creating incentives for businesses everywhere to produce more to take advantage of more easily accessible foreign markets. This is expected to generate more economic activity, jobs, and growth. According to the theory of 'comparative advantage' – that some countries are good at producing one thing (like cars), while other are good at producing another (like coffee) – every country is supposed to benefit from freer trade. This is less than clear in practice however, and a global controversy has emerged as to whether we are on the right track or not.

Barriers to trade are any policy measures that alter – or 'distort' – the uninhibited flow of trade. Typical barriers 'protect' domestic production from the competition of cheap imports, and thus are called 'protectionism'. Barriers can take the form of tariffs (taxes on imports), but there are many other forms; as a group they are called non-tariff barriers (NTBs). Non-tariff barriers can be import quotas, local content requirements, production subsidies and price supports (because they make local products more competitive than unsubsidized imports), export subsidies (because they confer an artificial advantage on foreign products in importing countries), and a myriad of others. Many NTBs are difficult to identify at first. Even health and quality standards and labelling requirements can act as barriers, as can rules orienting governments to purchase locally or to support local or minority-owned businesses.

When governments remove barriers to trade (like import tariffs and quotas), they are 'opening' their markets to foreign competitors. The risk they take is that domestic producers may be driven out of business if the imports are too cheap. If that is because the same good can be produced more cheaply elsewhere because of 'pure' comparative advantage – climatic conditions, for example – then theory postulates it would be better in any event to be producing something else, where the home country has a 'true' comparative advantage. The problem is that in the real world, as we shall see, cheaper products are rarely cheaper because of 'pure' comparative advantage, but rather because of 'distortions' like subsidies, according to popular misconception, or more usually, because of the effects of market concentration and misguided government policies. And comparative advantage at home, for a typical Third World country, may be nothing more than a lower-paid, more exploited workforce.

Historical context

As we examine the issues behind this global controversy, we do well to keep in mind the historical context of trade liberalization. World economic history has long been characterized by cycles – or pendulum swings – between freer trade and protectionism. Swings toward trade liberalization are sometimes referred to as 'economic integration' – as in 'integrating the economies of Canada, the US and Mexico via NAFTA' – and the most recent swing has been dubbed 'economic globalization'.

It would be erroneous to presume that integration and globalization have never happened before. The clearest historical example is that of European colonialism, in which the economies of the colonies were integrated into the increasingly global economies of Europe. That 'swing' ended during the last century in the period marked by the two world wars, when a combination of war, national independence of former colonies, and economic nationalism reversed a century of trade liberalization. This ushered in an era of relative protectionism, which was to be reversed again in the 1970s and 1980s.

In the 1970s, businesses in the United States and Europe began to confront crises brought on by rising wages at home and excess productive capacity. In other words, they now found themselves with the ability to produce more than home markets could absorb. They needed access to Third World markets to move their excess production. This brought the issue of protectionism by Third World governments to the fore, precisely at the same time as these same Southern governments became enmeshed in the debt crisis. This set the stage for the renegotiation of the debt in venues like the World Bank and the International Monetary Fund (IMF), where both Southern and Northern countries were represented.

Structural adjustment: precursor to trade agreements

The 'South' wanted debt restructuring, and the 'North' wanted greater access to Southern markets. The solution was debt restructuring conditioned upon the adoption of Structural Adjustment Packages (SAPs) by Southern governments. A central feature of these SAPs was trade liberalization, including the slashing of import tariffs and quotas, steep cuts in domestic subsidies, and the start of across-the-board privatization of state services and enterprises.[19] The heyday of SAPs began in the late 1970s and continued into the early 1990s. When we examine the impacts on Third World economies to date of trade liberalization, we cannot really separate the effects of liberalization through SAPs from the effects of liberalization through the WTO, NAFTA, or other trade agreements, as we shall see in the Mexico and Africa examples below. A central complaint of Southern governments in contemporary trade negotiations is that of 'asymmetry' – that they have already opened their markets unilaterally to a significant extent under SAPs, and now they are being pushed to engage in another round of tariff cuts via the WTO. Even if these are to be the same percentage cuts for Northern and Southern countries, or even if they give a slight advantage to the South, they will not erase already existing imbalances created by SAPs and by colonial legacies.

From GATT to the Uruguay Round and the WTO

Over the latter part of that period the central fulcrum for further trade liberalization shifted from debt negotiations to trade agreements and treaties. This began by giving more substance to GATT, which was originally negotiated in 1948 to shape the post-Second World War economy by regulating tariffs and other trade regulations. However, it had little power of enforcement, only addressed trade in goods (as opposed to trade in services, intellectual property rights like patents and copyrights, government purchasing policies, etcetera), and a significant part of the world's nations were not GATT signatories. Also notable was the exclusion of agriculture from GATT because of food security concerns.[20]

This was to change with the Uruguay Round, a series of trade talks which lasted from 1986 to 1994, and which expanded the rules of international trade to cover services, intellectual property and agriculture. A trade 'round' is the name given to series of negotiations where countries try to reach agreements on trade issues such as tariff reduction. The WTO was created during the Uruguay Round.

The WTO began life in 1995 as a new global commerce agency, transforming the old GATT into an enforceable global trade code. The stated objectives of the WTO include 'raising standards of living, ensuring full employment and a large and steadily growing volume of real income and effective demand, and expanding the production of and trade in goods and services', in other words, economic development based on the market. This means that WTO agreements are meant to introduce free market principles into international trade, via two basic mechanisms: (1) reducing trade barriers; and (2) applying nondiscriminatory rules (stronger countries should not have special advantages over weaker countries). An additional important principle, at least in theory, is special consideration for developing countries. The WTO recognizes 'that there is need for positive efforts designed to ensure that developing countries, and especially the least developed among them, secure a share in the growth of international trade commensurate with the needs of their economic development'.[21]

Every two years, give or take, the WTO holds its Ministerial meetings. At these meetings key decisions are taken regarding the future path of the WTO. Between Ministerials, ongoing negotiations continue within the so-called 'built-in agenda', which includes agriculture, services and intellectual property rights. The ongoing negotiations on trade in agricultural and food products are carried out under the rubric of the evolving Agreement on Agriculture (AoA), though there are also many non-AoA issues – like intellectual property, competition, investment and government procurement policies – that also impinge on agriculture.

Key recent events: agriculture is gumming up the works[22]

A lot of media attention, public debate, and protest has been focused on trade negotiations in recent years, especially surrounding the series of key events summarized here. It is notable, among all the controversy and failed summits, how central a role differences over agricultural trade issue have played in gumming up the works. Food and agriculture have proved to be the most significant stumbling blocks along the way to re-structuring the global trading system.

1994 – NAFTA enters into effect

The first day of 1994 marked the entry into effect of the North American Free Trade Area, a treaty that integrates the economies of Canada, the US and Mexico. In many ways NAFTA is the model trade agreement, including, as do other agreements, directly trade-related issues like import tariffs and quotas, but also many less directly trade-related issues like investment, and competition between domestic and foreign firms. NAFTA is the model of what the US and the EU are seeking – but have not yet achieved – in the WTO, of what the US wants from the proposed Free Trade Area of the Americas (FTAA), and of what the US has achieved in more recent bilateral and regional agreements with Chile, Central America (CAFTA), and others. NAFTA is often considered to be the 'laboratory' in which to study the anticipated effects of agreements that are still being negotiated (WTO, FTAA) or have just been signed (CAFTA). While NAFTA did open Mexico to a wave of foreign investment, it has been its negative impacts on rural peoples that have most thrown trade liberalization into question. Most spectacularly, 1 January 1994 was also marked by the rebellion of the Zapatistas in Chiapas, Mexico, who called NAFTA 'a death sentence for the indigenous people of México', because of its anticipated consequences for poor farmers.

1999 – *The WTO Seattle Ministerial*

The Third Ministerial of the WTO was held in in Seattle in 1999 amid massive demonstrations with tens of thousands of people taking to the streets against the policies of the WTO. This was the key event that put the issue of the impacts on globalization in the public eye. The Ministerial was supposed to make major advances on agricultural trade and intellectual property rights (essentially extending US-style patents and copyrights around the world), among other topics, but the talks collapsed as the combined result of the street demonstrations and differences between the US and EU on agriculture, as well as between the North and the South on agriculture, intellectual property, and the transparency of the process itself (77 countries walked out on the last day).

2001 – *the WTO Doha Ministerial*

The next Ministerial was held in 2001 in the Persian Gulf State of Qatar – a country which does not allow significant public protest or demonstrations. One again the negotiators reached no specific agreements, though the start of the Doha Round of negotiations was declared. In this new 'Development Round', the South agreed to consider adding 'new issues' to the WTO agenda – expanding its mandate to less directly trade-related topics – in exchange for the North agreeing that the WTO should give more attention to the concern of the South that trade liberalization, as practised so far, was already damaging their national economies (in other words, there should be more options for 'special' or 'differential' treatment for poor countries).

2002 – FTAA negotiations in Quito

Between Doha and the Fifth Ministerial, held in Cancún, Mexico in September 2003, no significant progress was made in negotiating any outstanding issues, neither in the WTO nor in the other major forum of trade negotiations, the proposed Free Trade Area of the Americas. In 2002 in Quito, Ecuador, agricultural trade issues, accompanied by massive street protests by organizations of farmers and indigenous people, blocked significant advances in negotiation toward the FTAA. As we have seen, after failing to reach agreement with Latin American trade ministers in Quito, US Trade Representative Robert Zoellick said that if the USA could not get what it needed from the FTAA negotiations, it would get it in the WTO.[23]

2003 – the WTO Cancún Ministerial

We have seen how, collapsing just as Seattle had, again stumbling over agriculture and marked by massive street protests and the self-immolation of Lee Kyung Hae, Cancún also marked the emergence of new Southern country negotiating blocs with agendas running counter to US and EU proposals.[24]

2003 – scaling back the FTAA in Miami

Following a scant two months after Cancún, widespread intransigence by Latin American governments, mostly around agriculture, essentially brought the FTAA as previously conceived to a halt. In a face-saving move, the US was forced to go along with heavily scaled-back plans for what the international media quickly called 'FTAA-lite.'[25]

2003–6 – A wave of smaller trade agreements

We have already seen that at the end of the Cancún meeting, Zoellick presaged the next stage of trade negotiations by announcing that the US would 'move towards free trade with can-do countries.'[26] Thus in the immediate aftermath of Cancún, both the

US and the EU signed a number of bilateral and regional agreements with more 'pliable' governments (the CAFTA arrangement
with Central America has already been cited) in lieu of progress in
the WTO or the FTAA.[27]

2004 – A July breakthrough for the WTO?

Then, in July of 2004, the WTO member nations took up negotiations again on a 'framework' for talks leading up to the expected
Sixth Ministerial to be held in 2005. The 'July framework,' which
was actually announced in August, was widely hailed as a break-
through, as the South agreed to restart negotiations on agriculture
and other issues in exchange for a promise by the US and the EU to
cut some of their subsidies. However, many observers questioned
the extent to which any real progress was made, despite the hype.

2005 – An agreement in Hong Kong to continue negotiating

At the Sixth Ministerial of the WTO, in Hong Kong in December
of 2005, the streets were filled with protesting farmers (2,000 from
South Korea alone, in memory of Lee Kyung Hae) and trade
unionists. Nevertheless, Brazil and India essentially turned their
backs on the rest of the Third World, gaining entry into the 'big
boys' club' by using their influence among the so-called G20
nations to gain acceptance for the July framework, and get the
stalled negotiations started again. Thus they served the interests of
the most powerful nations. With vague promises from the US and
Europe to cut subsidies by 2013, Southern countries made
concessions on further market opening.[28] The only real agreement
reached at Hong Kong, however, was to negotiate some more.

But, what's all the fuss about? Why has it been impossible for
governments to come to agreements about trade in agricultural
products, farm subsidies and related issues? And why are farmer
organizations up in arms?

2

Key Issues, Misconceptions, Disagreements and Alternative Paradigms

In order to sort out the confusion of often contradictory positions and misleading rhetoric from governments, it is useful to single out the key issues, highlighting where there are common misconceptions and the central points of disagreement between governments, and between governments and key elements in global civil society. The following list and short explanations serve as a useful guide to the larger debate. To see how these issues are actually incorporated, or ignored, in the WTO process, turn to **How the WTO Rules Agriculture** on p. 81. This section concludes with two alternative paradigms that have been posed as alternatives to the dominant trade liberalization model.

Key issues in current trade negotiations

There are a number of key issues that together constitute the terrain of the negotiations and disputes.

Market access

This is an issue for both Northern and Southern governments. As we saw in the historical review above, access to Southern country markets for US and European Union (EU) exports was a key motivation, first for SAPs and later for trade negotiations. On the

other hand, the asymmetry by which Northern countries currently
rely on a range of non-tariff trade barriers (NTBs) to offer greater
protection to their home markets than Southern countries are
permitted for theirs, has turned 'market access' to Northern
markets, for Southern exports, into a central rallying cry in the
current round of negotiations. This was the key point of consensus
that united the so-called G20 large Southern agro-export powers –
like Brazil, China, South Africa and India – in their blocking of new
agreements in Cancún (**Government Negotiating Blocs** and what
they stand for are outlined on p. 89). The endorsement of market
access at a rhetorical level by the US and EU, combined with their
unwillingness to offer hard concessions, was seen by G20
negotiators, and the international media, as hypocritical, helping
to torpedo the meetings (see **Box 2.1, Government Doublespeak
on Trade** on p. 27 for an example of government doublespeak on
these issues).

On the other hand, it is important to understand that the G20
and US/EU positions on market access are not so divergent in
reality, as seen by the way that Brazil and India switched horses, and
essentially took on the role of recruiting Third World nations to
sign on to US and European proposals in Hong Kong in 2005. The
G20 nations accept the trade liberalization paradigm, but feel it has
been applied unfairly to date, as they have been forced to liberalize
far more than Northern countries. As agro-export powers in their
own right, they want the same opportunity to benefit from this
pro-free trade model as the US and EU. Family farm and peasant
groups, on the other hand, hold a different position. Grouped
together in a global alliance called La Via Campesina that pools both
Northern and Southern farm groups, they place greater importance
on domestic markets, where the vast majority of the world's farm
production goes, than on export markets, and see a trade-off
between the two. Market opening helps agro-exporters, they agree,
but point out that these are but a tiny minority of the world's
farmers. On the other hand, market opening hurts the vast majority

Box 2.1 Government Doublespeak on Trade

Many governments, including that of the United States, have displayed rather unfortunate tendencies to speak about trade in euphemisms that disguise their real intentions. In the case of the US, because other countries and civil society actors – like farmer organizations and NGOs – have become skilled at the art of 'watch what they do, not what they say,' it has contributed to growing anti-American sentiment and hard feelings abut US doublespeak and hypocrisy on these issues. This is a small sample of how to decode US government statements about trade.

EXPLANATION: The countries with 'high tariffs' are poor counties, the countries with 'low tariffs' are rich countries. What this means is that the poor countries, who cannot affor significant domestic support, will lose one of the few affordable tools in their farm trade regulation toolbox: tariffs.

TRANSLATION: What we do [what the US does], will be called 'non-trade distorting', and what others do will be called 'trade distorting.' We will have unlimited rights, to do what we do, but what everyone else does will be severely limited.

THE MESSAGE: The US doesn't subsidize exports, only others do that (never mind that billions of dollars of US exports credits don't count in the definition!)

WHAT'S THIS ABOUT? 'State trading enterprises' include the marketing agencies that poor countries use to give peasant farmers access to markets. No 'disciplines' are proposed for the global grain trading corporations that replace them when they are shut down or privatized.

SO, WHAT HAPPENED LATER? The EU decided to convert their Blue Box programs into Green Box programs like the US has. Still later, the US and the EU got together to propose unlimited Blue Box programs (See How the WTO Rules Agriculture on p. 81).

Veneman outlines ambitious WTO proposal

Agriculture Online News, July 26, 2002

Nara, Japan – Ag Secretary Ann Veneman has outlined an ambitious US proposal for reforming the rules of global agricultural trade...

Veneman said the US proposal would substantially reduce global trade barriers, slash trade-distorting subsidies and eliminate export subsidies. Specifically, the US is calling for all WTO members to reduce all tariffs using a formula that would reduce high tariffs more than low tariffs and result in no tariff over 25% after 5 years...

Subsidies would be deemed either trade distorting or non-trade distorting. Non-trade distorting support remains without limit, but trade distorting support would be capped at 5% of a country's value of agriculture output. The proposed calls for elimination of export subsidies over 5 years, phased down in equal amounts, and new disciplines on state trading enterprises.

Currently, the EU can support its farmers at a rate that is approximately 25% of the value of its agricultural production. Japan can provide support equal to 40% of its value of production, but the US is limited to less than 10% of the value of its production. In addition, USDA says, the EU spends over $20 billion in trade distorting 'blue box' programs while the US spends zero.

of farmers who produce for domestic markets, as they are now subject to unfair competition from artificially cheap imports.

Domestic subsidies

Domestic subsidies are government payments and services to farmers and agribusinesses, and are sometimes confused with domestic supports, which is a broader category that also includes mechanisms to boost crop and livestock prices, like import tariffs and quotas, and price supports. In the dominant WTO paradigm, subsidies are divided into those that potentially distort trade by paying for producing products destined for export that might not otherwise be produced – like payments to farmers that increase as a farmer produces more – and subsidies that do not distort trade. An example of the latter would be payments for soil conservation, or payments to take land out of production. The conventional wisdom on subsidies – especially the market-distorting category – is that they are the principle source of unfairness in the global system of agricultural trade. Richer countries can, and in fact have afforded, vastly higher levels of subsidies than poorer countries. Thus their production is greater than it would be without these payments, and their products can be sold in world markets at lower prices because the payments can compensate farmers for low or negative profit margins.

While the US and EU officially endorse slashing subsidies, in practice they have been very reluctant to do so, and have often resorted to what critics and Southern governments perceive as 'disguising' trade-distorting subsidies as non-trade-distorting ones (see **How the WTO Rules Agriculture** on p. 81). Thus the subsidy issue has played a key role in many failed trade summits. Farmer organizations, on the other hand, and many trade economists, see the subsidy issue very differently. They point to studies showing that even if all Northern trade-distorting subsidies were removed tomorrow, excessively low crop and livestock prices would still pervade global commodity markets. Just as importantly, farm

don't all have same impact or use

must make distinction btwn purposes of subsidies

groups make a critical, yet often overlooked, distinction between what might be termed 'inappropriate and wasteful subsidies,' and other components of public sector services and budgets that need to be maintained or boosted for legitimate environmental, economic and rural development purposes, and to maintain the fundamental viability of farming as an economic, social and cultural activity. Unfortunately, say farmers, the current tendency is to 'throw the baby out with the bathwater,' as legitimate government services are typically lumped with wasteful practices under the rubric of 'subsidies' to be slashed or eliminated.

Export subsidies

This is another major bone of contention, but one in which apparent US and EU concessions recently helped re-start stalled WTO negotiations. These nations, especially the EU, have massive subsidies for exporters (largely agribusinesses and not farmers), which are heavily trade-distorting. The US has long used export credits – not included in the WTO's technical definition of export subsidies – to 'evade' the export subsidy issue and point the finger at the EU. In the 2004 July framework, however, the US in principle accepted the possibility of reclassifying these credits as export subsidies, and both the US and EU agreed in Hong Kong to place the possible elimination of all export subsidies on the negotiating table, though there are major doubts as to their sincerity and as to the real likelihood of these proposed cuts.

Dumping

Although there are technical disagreements and confusion over its definition, in general 'dumping' refers to the export of products to third countries at prices below the cost of production, though sometimes it has been defined as prices below those in the home market. The point is that when foreign products enter a local market at prices below the cost of production, local farmers cannot compete and are driven off the land and into deepening poverty. It is thus classified as a prohibited, anti-competitive practice by the WTO. However, loopholes in the technical definitions, and very costly and bureaucratic procedures for enforcement, have meant that typical anti-dumping cases are brought by the US or the EU, and rarely by poorer countries, despite the widespread perception and underlying reality that the latter are the more frequent victims of dumping, especially when it comes to food and agriculture.

While Southern country governments see dumping as a very important issue, they give it lower priority than market access and subsidies in the actual negotiations. This highlights a critical distinction within the broader category of farmers, and an underlying difference in access to the levers of political power. Every country in the Third World is characterized by a large number of farmers – typically, but not just, peasants – who produce for their domestic markets and whose livelihoods are severely impaired by dumping, and a far smaller number of wealthier farmers who produce for export and who stand to gain from greater market access and cuts in subsidies in the North. Thus the Via Campesina accuses many Southern governments, particularly those in the G20, of pandering to tiny but wealthy and politically powerful agro-export elites when they give up on anti-dumping controls in exchange for Northern concessions on market access and subsidies.

A critical issue concerning dumping has to do with the specific mechanisms that cause it. While subsidies may have driven dumping in the past, some recent academic studies suggest that market concentration, and the virtual elimination of supply management and price support policies in the US and Europe, are far more important today in keeping crop and livestock prices down. Over the past twenty years a few companies have come to buy the bulk of what farmers produce in each of many key commodities, and they use their market power to keep the price they pay as low as possible, enabling them to turn around and dump the same products in foreign markets at prices below the cost of production. At the same time, the US and Europe have changed their farm policies, de-emphasizing supply management (which once reduced overproduction) and price supports (which put a floor on how low prices could go).

Market concentration

If we are serious about addressing the problems associated with dumping, then the issue of monopolies and oligopolies – not currently on the negotiation table – will need to be addressed. Farmer organizations are clear on this point, but to date governments have not seriously addressed it in the context of agricultural trade.

Special and differential treatment/special safeguards

Most governments in the South argue that the WTO has not lived up to the commitment in its charter to make 'positive efforts' to ensure that developing countries, and especially the poorest countries, known collectively as the least-developed countries (LDCs), receive some benefit from the global trading system. They demand that poor countries receive 'special' and 'differential' treatment to compensate for their disadvantages. The G33 countries, none of whom are agro-export powers, call for what used to be called a 'Development Box,' which is the ability for poorer countries to designate 'Special Products' (SPs) whose protection from cheap imports is critical for economic and rural development, food security and anti-poverty objectives. They would not be required to cut tariffs on such agricultural products. They also call for a 'Special Safeguard Mechanism' (SSM), which would allow them to invoke special tariffs if there were major import surges in any product, 'special' or not, that threatened their domestic economy. Taken together, SPs and the SSM are 'special safeguards.' The G90 countries, a coalition of African, Caribbean, Pacific and LDC countries, support the G33 position on SP/SSM, and also the G20 position on market access and Northern subsidies. The US and EU also support SP/SSM, though in a milder version, and especially want to have the right themselves to designate SPs and to invoke an SSM against import surges of exports from the South. Farmer organizations criticize the Development Box or SP/SSM position for being too weak, and for essentially accepting the trade liberalization paradigm, albeit with some 'fine tuning.'

Other issues with an impact on food and agriculture

Though they are not dealt with in depth in this book, there are a number of other polemical issues on the bargaining table in trade talks that also affect agriculture and rural areas. One such area is food quality and safety, which represents a major split between the US and EU, the latter joined by many Southern countries. The US position, backed by WTO rules, is that while countries can discriminate against dangerous products based on 'sound science,' that such discrimination can only apply to the final product itself and not to the process used to produce it. Both the 'science' issue and the 'production process' issue have caused friction. Most countries and people believe that when science cannot tell us how serious a risk is, then we should be cautious, though the US opposes this principle in international negotiations. The US claims that the 'precautionary principle' backed by other countries to discriminate against products whose health and environmental safety are still largely unstudied – like genetically engineered (GE) foods, or beef produced with growth hormones, is not 'science-based' because 'scientific evidence' is still lacking. In terms of the 'production process,' we might also imagine a hypothetical case where 'scientific evidence' were to appear that showed that GE foods were not a consumer risk, but that GE crops are an ecological risk where they are grown. In such a case, the US might well fight against barring a product on that basis, because it would be based on the production process (growing crops) and not on the final product itself (a food item). Another wedge issue, this time between the US and EU on the one hand, and the Third World on the other, is that of Intellectual Property Rights (IPRs), which are addressed in the

Trade-Related Aspects of Intellectual Property Rights (TRIPS) negotiations in the WTO, and which are conducted separately from the agriculture negotiations. In terms of agriculture, this means that the rest of the world should accept US-style patent protection, or 'plant variety protection,' and thus farmers everywhere should have to pay royalties for using crop varieties patented by foreign corporations. While Third World governments have largely accepted TRIPS at the rhetorical level, they are engaged in a massive passive resistance comprised of foot dragging on national legislation required by the WTO. In general, family farm, peasant, environmentalist, consumer, indigenous, and labor organizations worldwide back the precautionary principle and oppose TRIPS.

Alternative paradigms

Two significant alternatives to the agricultural liberalization paradigm have been put forward, both with significant impacts. These are considered below.

Multifunctionality

According to this concept,[29] agriculture is not just about producing tradable commodities, but rather has multiple functions in society. It is also about preserving landscapes and protecting farm livelihoods and rural traditions, and it is about food security, and thus deserves special consideration in trade agreements, according to the proponents of this concept.[30] Multifunctionality was originally championed by the EU, as a way to justify maintaining subsidies for European farmers. The EU sought an alliance with the Third World nations on this concept, but the US and Cairns Group (a now mostly defunct bloc of major agro-exporting countries) successfully argued that the EU was guilty of hypocritically defending its own farmers while subsidizing exports that undercut farmers elsewhere, thus blocking support for this concept from Southern nations. Of course cheap agroexports from the US and Cairns also damaged the ability

of other farmers to make a living, but nevertheless the EU
eventually stopped talking about multifunctionality. But the
concept is still defended by another group of nations, the G10
countries, who are mainly relatively developed countries like
Taiwan, South Korea, Norway and Switzerland, who are not
significant agroexporters but who have major small-farmer-based
rural economies. They defend, among other things, the economic
and cultural integrity of their rural regions, and value their
countrysides and food quality highly. They are also concerned with
price fluctuations. For Japan, Korea and Norway, whose food is
largely imported, food security is regarded as a public good. To
them it would be unacceptable to make their food supply totally
dependent on the vagaries of the international market, or on
political or economic pressures. The irrigated rice countries, like
Japan and Korea, additionally stress the relationship between
agriculture and the environment, through the rice paddy landscape.
According to the G10, these considerations justify an active role for
government in the regulation of externalities and in the production
of public goods, and these concerns have made the G10 into a
minor yet significant player in trade negotiations.

Peoples' food sovereignty

The concept of food sovereignty was developed by La Via
Campesina,[31] and brought to the public debate during the World
Food Summit in 1996 as an alternative paradigm in which to frame
issues about food and agriculture. Since that time the concept has
gained tremendous popularity and resonance in civil society sectors
of nations both North and South, and has been developed into a
holistic and internally coherent alternative framework.[32] Like the
concept of multifunctionality, it is based on the 'special' nature of
agriculture (as compared to industry, for example).

Food sovereignty proponents argue that food and farming are
about more than trade, and that production for local and national
markets is more important than production for export from various

perspectives: broad–based and inclusive local and national economic development, addressing poverty and hunger; preserving rural life, economies, and environments; and managing natural resources in a sustainable fashion. They argue that every country and people must have the right and the ability to define their own food, farming, and agricultural policies; to protect domestic markets; and to have public sector budgets for agriculture that may include subsidies provided these do not lead to greater production, exports, dumping and damage to other countries. They believe that low prices are the worst force that farmers face everywhere in the world, and there-fore that we need an effective ban on dumping; anti–monopoly rules that can be applied nationally and globally; the effective regulation of over-production in the large agro-export countries; and the elimination of all those direct and indirect, open and hidden subsidies that enforce low prices and over-production. In other words, that we need to move from mechanisms that enforce low prices to those that would promote fair prices for farmers and consumers alike. This alternative model also includes agrarian reform, with limits on maximum farm size, equitable local control over resources like seeds, land, water and forests, and firm opposition to patenting seeds. The food sovereignty approach is being taken increasingly seriously by researchers and other experts,[33] and forms the basis for collaboration between the Food and Agriculture Organization (FAO) of the UN and farmer groups and other civil society actors, announced by FAO Secretary-General Jacques Diouf at the 2002 World Food Summit.[34]

3

Dumping and Subsidies:
Unraveling the Confusion

The confusing case of Ol' King Cotton

Cotton prices are hugely distorted by subsidies. It may well be a case where the common perception that subsidies cause dumping has some truth, though the most serious problems of over-supply in global markets began when the US ended supply management of cotton in 1996.[35] And the way the much-publicized case has played out may actually make the kinds of alternatives envisioned by farmer organizations harder to achieve. [36]

According to the Overseas Development Institute, more than one-fifth of the value of world cotton production comes from government subsidies, principally in the US, China and the EU.[37] In the US, for example, 2001–2 subsidies totaled some US$2.3 billion, while the EU provided US$700 million and China US$1.2 billion. These subsidies encourage excess cotton production, which is then dumped on the world market at prices below the cost of production. This has driven down world cotton prices, severely hurting a number of poor countries which rely on exports of cotton as a substantial portion of their foreign exchange earnings. Chad, Burkina Faso, Mali and Benin brought this issue to the fore at Cancún. In these countries cotton accounts for 5–10 per cent of GDP, more than one-third of total export earnings, and more than two-thirds of the value of their agricultural exports. In Cancún they proposed that subsidies be gradually phased out, with transitional measures to ease the burden of lost revenues borne by least-developed countries (LDCs). While their proposal received a lot of media attention, it was eventually lost in the shuffle at the actual negotiations. In Hong Kong they had to celebrate as 'victory' a weak agreement that essentially bought the US more time on the same issue.[38]

In 2003 a much less poor country, Brazil, formally challenged US cotton subsidies at the WTO, and later the WTO issued a preliminary ruling in Brazil's favor, accepting the general form of the argument that domestic subsidies and supports distort trade.[39] Brazil accused the US of violating a WTO cap of US$1.6 billion/ year on cotton subsidies, and of providing an additional US$1.7 billion in credits to US manufacturers and agribusinesses to buy American cotton. According to Brazil, without these illegal subsidies, US cotton production – which currently holds a 40% global market share – would have fallen by 29 per cent, and US cotton exports by 41 per cent, leading to a rise of 12.6 per cent in the world price of cotton, benefiting Brazilian producers. The US contended that cotton subsidies are not directly linked to production, and thus are not illegal under the WTO, calling them domestic supports that do not harm international markets.

The WTO decision on this matter has been widely hailed as the first nail in the coffin of farm subsidies, with challenges to domestic supports for other commodities to follow soon. As such, a broad spectrum of opinion, ranging from Third World governments to the *New York Times*, has seen the decision in a positive light.[40]

On the other hand, family farm organizations, like those in La Via Campesina, have tended to see the decision in a more negative light. They say it identified too broad a variety of subsidies and domestic supports as potentially illegal, and could open the door to challenges not just to wasteful and inappropriate subsidies, but to essential services and supports as well.

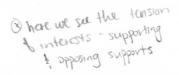

Paul Nicholson, a leading European family farmer spokesman and a member of the International Coordinating Committee of Via Campesina,[41] says that while this decision appears at first glance to be positive, coming as it did against the US, farmer organizations view it as a grave precedent. Farmers everywhere, North and South, need public sector budgets for agriculture and for rural development – subsidies, in other words – and the decision was potentially so broad as to permit attacks on all kinds of subsidies, not just 'bad' ones. The farmer position is that subsidies *per se* are not the enemy. Their merit depends on how much the subsidies cost, who gets them, and what they pay for.

(handwritten margin note) do they need public support?

Farm subsidies: who gets them?

In both the US and the EU, farm subsidies payments are biased toward the largest and wealthiest farmers, who in many cases are not farmers at all, but rather companies. In both cases they function to compensate farmers for low crop prices, so that instead of decreasing the area planted to a given crop when the price drops, larger farm operations maintain or even increase the area planted. The result is to short circuit the normal tendency toward reduced area which would otherwise lead prices to rise again. Instead, there is nothing to keep prices from falling and falling, which is exactly what they have done.

In the United States, farm subsidies totaled US$114 billion between 1995 and 2002, an average of US$14.25 billion per year. Of that total, about 80 per cent went to support the incomes of farmers and companies mostly engaged in crop farming. Another 12.5 per cent was in the form of so-called 'conservation programs' (which vary in the extent to which they really achieve conservation objectives), while some 7 per cent was paid out in disaster programs, in response to bad weather.[42] While the wealthiest 1 per cent of growers received an average annual payment of $214,088, the 20th percentile (still the wealthiest fifth of all farmers) averaged

Table 3.1 Distribution of US Farm Payments, 2003

Per cent of recipients	Average payment per percentile
Top 1%	$214,088
Top 2%	$86,500
Top 3%	$62,358
Top 4%	$50,311
Top 5%	$42,656
Top 6%	$37,108
Top 7%	$32,657
Top 8%	$28,987
Top 9%	$25,924
Top 10%	$23,352
Top 11%	$21,149
Top 12%	$19,927
Top 13%	$17,573
Top 14%	$16,102
Top 15%	$14,783
Top 16%	$13,598
Top 17%	$12,529
Top 18%	$11,575
Top 19%	$10,710
Top 20%	$9,916

Source: Wise, 2005a.

just $9,916 (see Table 3.1), and the rest got much less, or none. Typical American farmers found themselves mired in debt as a result of low prices and high production costs (see Figure 3.1).

In 2002 the US approved a new farm bill, the so-called Farm Security and Rural Investment Act, which extended the basic US subsidy system for another ten years, at an estimated cost to taxpayers of US$190 billion. Coming as it did while the world was enmeshed in negotiations over farm trade, this was widely seen as a slap in the face for Third World governments.[43]

In the EU, the distribution of subsidies is not much better than

Food is Different

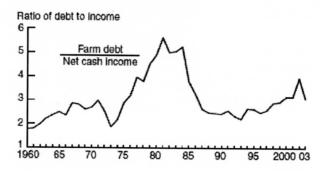

Figure 3.1 Total farm sector debt compared with net cash farm income, 1960–2003

Source: Stam and Dixon, 2004.

in the US. Some 78 per cent of the 5.2 million beneficiaries of the Common Agricultural Policy (CAP) receive less than 5,000 Euros a year (US$6,000), while 1.8 per cent of recipients receive some €500,000 or above,[44] driving an estimated 120,000 mostly family-sized farmers per year (more than 2,000 per week) to lose their farms as a result of low prices.[45]

But beyond the unequal way in which payments are handed out, the real tragedy is that (with a few exceptions) they no longer play a role in limiting overproduction, nor in providing minimum prices to farmers, thus allowing the prices that farmers get for their crops and livestock to fall ever lower. The main winners from these policies are corporate livestock operations who buy absurdly cheap feed, making environmentally destructive factory farming possible,[46] and the big US and European agro-exporters who buy their raw materials so cheaply that they can out-compete any local producer in their home market.

In the family farmer view, subsidies paid only to large corporate producers in the North, leading to dumping and the destruction of rural livelihoods in the Third World, are bad. But subsidies paid to family farmers to keep them on the land and to support vibrant rural economies, and subsidies that assist with soil conservation, the transition to sustainable farming practices, and direct marketing to local consumers, are good. The real enemy of farmers is low prices. And farm gate prices – what farmers receive – continue to drop even while consumer prices rise. This is consistent with the hypothesis that market concentration, and the lack of supply management and price supports, are what keep prices low by and large, as corporations wield their economic and market power to influence public policy and to buy cheap from farmers and sell dear to consumers.[47]

A leading US non-governmental organization, the Institute for Agriculture and Trade Policy (IATP), takes the position that, while the WTO cotton ruling may be questionable, it may still be useful in bringing the issue of dumping to the fore:

> This case will not solve the problem of agricultural dumping, but it should jumpstart a discussion on how to lift prices paid to farmers, which would cut subsidies and stop dumping. Dumping is caused by over-supply. Farmers will over-produce when prices go down, and they'll over-produce whether they receive subsidies or not. This ruling begs for a comprehensive agricultural inventory management program to bring supply into balance with demand, and ensure farmers are paid a fair price.[48]

In other words, the cotton ruling may not be the correct decision, but it most definitely highlights the need to go back to the drawing board on issues of farm policy and agricultural trade.

Dumping and subsidies

Throughout the Third World, dumping is what is driving millions of farmers off the land and into urban slums and international migratory streams. It causes the low crop prices that make earning a livelihood off the land increasingly impossible.[49] It is also illegal under well-established international rules. Yet because of the way these rules are written, they are virtually unenforceable when the complainant is a poor country. First, countries must scientifically establish harm, often a difficult task when reliable and timely statistics are not maintained. When the affected population is spread out over a national territory and not effectively represented, it is even harder. Second, political realities work against even filing cases. As the IATP argues:

> Underlying these technical problems is the political reality of the multilateral trading system. When the ultimate threat is the imposition of sanctions – the suspension of trade – then the tool is a lot easier to apply when the US challenges Bangladesh than vice versa. Just under half of Bangladesh's exports are destined for the USA; this isn't a trade relationship Bangladesh can afford to jeopardize. This dependence is of course not reciprocal, leaving the US with considerable leverage over what trade policy course Bangladesh follows.[50]

By far the best estimates available of the degree of dumping in global markets come from the work of the IATP.[51] According to their data, in 2002, a typical year, US exports were sold at average prices well below the cost of production.[52] For example:

- wheat was exported at an average price of 43 per cent below cost of production;
- soybeans were exported at an average price of 25 per cent below cost of production;
- maize was exported at an average price of 13 per cent below cost of production;
- cotton was exported at an average price of 61 per cent below cost of production;
- rice was exported at an average price of 35 per cent below cost of production.

While dumping is in fact the major problem of the current international trade regime in farm products – the media focus on US and EU subsidies may be off the mark. The confusion over sub–

sidies and dumping has intentionally or unintentionally extended to the Cairns group nations, to the G20 negotiating bloc, and to entities and people as diverse as the World Bank,[53] Oxfam, Jacques Diouf of FAO, Kofi Annan (head of the UN), the *Wall Street Journal*, and leading mainstream economists.[54] A lot of confusion and media hype has been associated with a widely circulated estimate of $300 billion per year in wealthy country subsidies, a figure popularized by the *New York Times* in the famous 2003 'Harvesting Poverty' series.[55] However, this figure is a major overestimate, as it conflates direct government payments with categories of what are more correctly called 'supports,' like the dollar value to farmers of policies that involve little or no government payments and actually raise rather than lower prices. [Note that farm policy in most countries is a mixture of wildly contradictory policies.] The correct figure for actual subsidies is no more than 30 per cent of the $300 figure.[56]

While dumping is what makes it impossible for Third World farmers to compete in their own home markets, today it is *not* largely caused by subsidies. This may not be immediately obvious, as statements about, for example, 'subsidized American maize flooding into Mexico undercut peasant production' make such logical sense. Yet blaming subsidies for low commodity prices is actually to reverse cause and effect. Especially after the 1996 and 2002 US Farm Bills, and the 2003 reform of the Common Agricultural Policy (CAP) in the EU, subsidies are largely *triggered* by low prices, in the form of emergency payments, counter-cyclical payments, etcetera. Where farm policy once included efforts to limit overproduction and keep prices from falling too low, virtually all brakes have now been removed on how low prices can drop, or on how much surplus can be produced. Emergency payments are given to farmers when prices fall so low that an economic emergency is declared in rural areas, though these payments are rarer and rarer these days. Counter-cyclical payments are designed to counter the normal 'hill and valley' cycles of rising and falling crop prices by filling in the

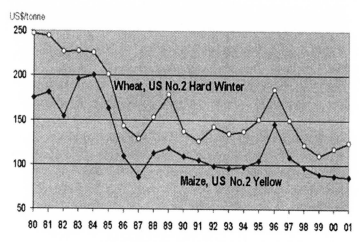

Figure 3.2 Global price trends for wheat and maize, corrected for inflation

Source: FAO, 2003.

valleys, kicking in when prices drop below average levels. In both cases government outlays go up in response to falling prices.

In other words, when farm prices rise, subsidies drop, and when prices drop, subsidies rise. The cause is the price, and the effect is the subsidy. Widely circulated economic simulation models run by Daryll Ray, Daniel De La Torre and Kelly Tiller at the University of Tennessee,[57] as well as models run by others,[58] clearly show that even the complete removal of subsidies would not have a very significant effect in raising chronically low farm prices, which are typically below the cost of production for most farmers, for most products, in most countries, and in most years. Figures 3.2 and 3.3 show examples of this global trend toward lower prices for farmers, whether they produce crops or livestock. So while the current US and EU subsidy systems are clearly misguided and unfair, and absolutely must be reformed, they are not today the root of the problem.

What then is the true cause of farm prices so chronically low that

1990–92 = 100

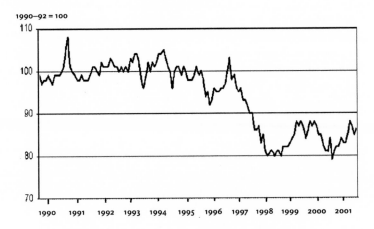

Figure 3.3 Index of world market price for meat
Source: FAO, 2003.

farmers cannot survive anywhere, North or South, without com-
pensatory subsidies? First, the shifts in farm policy in the US and the
EU, away from price supports and supply management (essentially
limits on overproduction), have allowed prices to fall almost
continuously. According to George Naylor, President of the
National Family Farm Coalition (NFFC):

> In the US, with the exception of a few cases of export sub-
> sidies or credits, corn, soybeans, wheat, etc. leave our shores
> at the same price as the farmer gets (with shipping and
> handling added on of course). That's why in order to stop
> dumping from the US, you need a price support and supply
> management system. Simply cutting subsidies won't do it.[59]

Second, over the past twenty years, concentration in the control
over agricultural markets has reached levels that most mainstream
economists in both developing and developed countries would
consider excessive by almost any measure. Many of the world's best

analysts of commodity prices believe that these high levels of concentration affect prices.[60] Clearly, integrated agri-food conglomerates have a vested interest in paying as little as possible for their raw
materials (crops and livestock), while charging as much as they can
to consumers.

Some examples from the US give an idea of the degree of
concentration that exists today:[61]

- Four companies – Cargill, Cenex Harvest States, Archer
  Daniels Midland (ADM), and General Mills – own 60 per cent
  of terminal grain handling facilities.
- Three companies (Cargill, ADM, and Zen Noh) carry out 82
  per cent of corn exporting.
- Four companies (Tyson, ConAgra, Cargill, and Farmland
  Nation) concentrate 81 per cent of the beef-packing industry.
- Four companies (ADM, ConAgra, Cargill, and General Mills)
  own 61 per cent of flour milling capacity.

Often the same companies are the dominant firms in several sectors.
ConAgra, for instance, figures among the four largest firms in the
beef, pork, turkey, sheep, and seafood sectors, with operations in 70
countries.[62]

How does concentration affect prices? Imagine a farmer in the
US Midwest growing a cereal crop some twenty years ago. He or
she might easily have had a choice of ten or more independent
elevators to sell their grain to, making it possible to shop around for
the best price, and making the buyers compete to some extent by
offering better prices. Today that same farmer most likely faces a
single corporate buyer who buys everything from all the local
elevators in their county. These are called 'captive draw areas.' A
corporate buyer with a captive draw area is free to set the price as
low as he likes, since there are no competing buyers. Beyond that
local affect, big players in global markets have the ability to
manipulate futures markets, and thus prices, to their advantage.[63]

These companies are very significant beneficiaries when prices

---

Box 3.1 Who Negotiates Agricultural Trade?[64]

It is interesting to ask who negotiates agricultural trade agreements and policies on behalf of the US government, in venues like the WTO, NAFTA and FTAA.[65] Ambassador Richard T. Crowder is the Chief Agricultural Negotiator at the USTR, the Office of the US Trade Representative. As such, he is charged with developing and putting forth the official positions of the US government on agricultural issues in all trade negotiations. Yet his background prior to joining the USTR raises the question of whether he in fact is 'industry's man' on agricultural trade, and if this is another case of the 'revolving door' between industry and government.

According to his official biography, before joining USTR he had been president and CEO of the American Seed Trade Association in Alexandria, Virginia, since 2002.[66] Prior to that, he worked as an independent consultant for a few years. From 1994 to 1999 he was Senior Vice-President (International) of DEKALB Genetics Corporation (now part of Monsanto), a worldwide leader in agricultural genetics and seed biotechnology. In this role he managed all of DEKALB's business outside the United States, involving more than 30 countries.

Before joining DEKALB in 1994, he was Executive Vice-President and General Manager, International of meat processor Armour Swift-Eckrich, a division of ConAgra. Before that, he served as Under-Secretary of International Affairs and Commodity Programs for the US Department of Agriculture from 1989 to 1992. In this role, he was responsible for all agencies concerned with international trade and development as well as domestic farm programs. He also played leadership roles in negotiating agriculture in the Uruguay Round of the GATT and in managing the 1990 Farm Bill process.

In the period 1975–89, he worked at the Pillsbury Company in a series of increasingly responsible senior executive positions. In other words, he has been back and forth several times between industry and government, and it is he who negotiated agricultural trade policies.

(handwritten) interesting, but maybe not relevant, nor surprising — a common occurrence

are low.[67] They, and others like them, are able to buy cheap in the
US and the EU, and thus undercut local producers at dumping
prices in markets around the world. As a result, prices in the US or
the EU, depending on the product in question, are, *de facto*, the
virtual world prices.[68] Once farmers everywhere are put in global
competition to sell to the same handful of companies, who dictate
low prices everywhere, the sad 'winners' among the farmers are
those who sell for the least, working 18–20 hour days, and scrimping
on all family expenditures. Dumping drives prices down worldwide,
such that the same companies can buy cheaply almost anywhere,
whether or not a given country has significant subsidies or not.

In a sense, concentrated corporate power is the root cause of low
prices through its ability both to dictate prices and to influence
policy. In the US, agribusiness has a long and sordid history of
influence peddling in the policy-making process,[69] and when subsidy
policy changes to remove the brakes on falling prices, or trade
policy changes to force markets open, it is not hard to imagine who
is behind it (see **Box 3.1, Who Negotiates Agricultural Trade?** on
p. 47).

George Naylor says, with a lot of common sense, that it is the
'penury of the market' that keeps farmers poor in both Northern
and Southern countries.[70] In other words, an unregulated market
exhibits both a tendency toward wild price swings and a tendency
toward ever lower prices as farmers must produce more just to keep
up. Of course, even worse is government and corporate interfer-
ence to drive prices even lower. We clearly do need regulation of
the market, but not the kind we currently have. In the last chapter
of this book we look at some positive alternatives.

While it is the market itself, plus concentration, and the concentrated economic and political power that goes with it, that are
behind keeping crop and livestock prices low, current-version
subsidies do play a role in that they allow the system to persist. On
the one hand, they no longer contain significant price support or
supply management mechanisms, while, on the other, they make it

possible for the key suppliers (large farmers in the US and EU) of these companies to keep supplying them, despite receiving prices below their costs of production.

Large growers are compensated with direct payments for producing at such low prices, while family farmers, the vast majority, get virtually nothing, and many are driven out of business. Sadly, not only does this system make it hard for Third World farmers who produce these commodities to compete in their own local and national markets, but it hurts most American farmers as well. One might say that these prices reflect 'internal dumping' for America's family farmers, as prices have fallen on the internal US market by an average of 40 per cent since 1996.[71]

What has been the result? In just five years, from 1997 to 2002, the US lost more than 90,000 farms of less than 2,000 acres, while farms above 2,000 acres increased by more than 3,600, according to the US Department of Agriculture, as cited by the IATP.[72]

As the IATP analysts put it:

> While the US government has put in place support programs to make up some of the income farmers lose from low prices, it is seldom enough. Larger, corporate farms receive the bulk of subsidy payments. In the US, the steady erosion of independent family farms, the near-necessity of off-farm income to ensure a farm family can continue to farm, and the decline in net farm income, all point to the cost of policies that facilitate the sale of commodities at less than cost of production prices.[73]

The result? An epidemic of farmer suicides across America,[74] often disguised as farm machinery accidents, so surviving family members can collect on life insurance, and either hang on to the family farm or get a head start on urban life.

Thanks to corporate near-monopolies, consumers do not benefit from low farm prices either, as is shown in Figure 3.4 by the relationship between consumer spending on food and what farmers get paid. As consumers pay more and more, farmers get less and less.

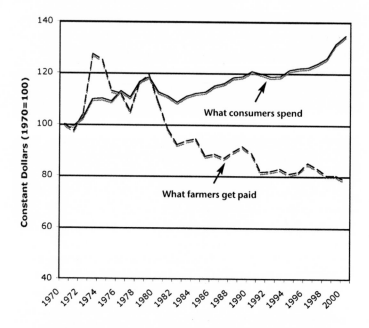

Figure 3.4 Spread of Food Spending vs Farm Value, US

Source: USDA, Economic Research Service.

A final word on subsidies in Northern countries. They may not be around forever. Remember that agribusiness companies exercise 'undue' influence on the negotiating positions of the US and the EU. What that might mean is that, as these companies come to depend less and less on US/EU subsidies – since if farmers there go out of business, they can always buy the same soy beans just as cheaply in Brazil, for example – we may see the government negotiators who are beholden to them increasingly make concessions in terms of cutting subsidies in exchange for further market opening, which is what these companies need most. In this context, it should come as no surprise that 'market access' is the buzz word of government negotiators from nations North and South.

The US and the EU push for greater market opening, gaining more access to the markets of the South, and the governments of the South call for greater market opening in the North – all of which eases the way for even more dumping. What this is all leading to, metaphorically, is a world in which nobody eats what is produced in their own country, where consumers in the US and EU dine on the products of the South, while consumers in the South eat only farm products exported from the North! A world where the world price – the dumping price – is the price everywhere, so that only the largest farmers can survive using volume to compensate for low per unit prices, yet where consumers fail to benefit because the 'free market' has allowed a few companies to gain control over everything and buy low and sell high. Far-fetched? Maybe not. Certainly the US and EU negotiators are still longing for ways to play 'hide the subsidy,' though they did agree to putative future cuts in Hong Kong.

But – to reiterate the central point of this chapter – eliminating subsidies won't mean better prices for farmers or for consumers, because market concentration will still enable companies to dictate low prices to farmers and high prices to consumers. In the final chapter of this book we will take a look at some alternative solutions that would be in the best interests of everyone – except, of course, the agribusiness corporations. But first, in the next chapter we look at the impacts on Southern nations of 'business as usual.'

4

The Impacts of
Liberalized Agricultural Trade

Taken from the broadest possible view, that of economic development, the wave of trade liberalization over the past three decades of world history has served to intensify already existing problems of poverty and underdevelopment, and to truncate the possibilities that the South has at its disposal to follow alternative development trajectories.[75] The nations of the South are deeply enmeshed in a rural crisis of epic proportions, and the market opening and subsequent dumping brought about by trade liberalization, first through SAPs and later through trade agreements, has been exactly the wrong medicine and its adverse effects have been compounded by 'non-trade-related' changes mandated as part of liberalization, including privatization and massive public sector budget cuts.

Liberalized agricultural trade, like liberalized trade in general, is meant to boost economic growth. Yet at the level of national economies, the idea that trade liberalization and 'openness' actually lead to economic growth in practice has come under increasing attack from economists in recent years.[76] At the broadest scale, studies conducted at the Center for Economic and Policy Research in Washington reveal that rates of economic growth in the South have been much lower during the decades of liberalization (from the mid-1970s on) than in prior decades (the earlier part of the post-war period). They also project the likely gains and losses to the

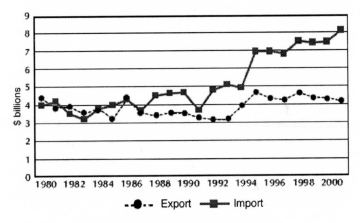

Figure 4.1 Food exports and imports of least-developed countries (LDCs), 1980–2001

Source: After UNCTAD, 2004.

South from further liberalization, and find that the South would gain much less from market access in the North than it would lose from giving up more access to its own markets.[77]

A recent empirical study published in the prestigious *Journal of Development Economics* shows that, on the average, greater market opening in the South has been associated with less economic growth. More specifically, the studies show that tariffs and non-tariff trade barriers actually promote growth in poorer countries, while removing them impedes growth.[78] This happens via the mechanism of the cheap imports that undercut local enterprises.

On the specific subject of trade in food and agricultural products, data from the United Nations Conference on Trade and Development (UNCTAD) shows that trade liberalization, and the dumping of farm products that inevitably follows, has generated a growing dependency on food imports in LDCs, as shown in Figure 4.1. The excess of imports over exports is a good proxy for the impact on the livelihoods of local farmers, who are typically squeezed out of their own national markets for food – markets they dominated in the past

– thus deepening the social and economic dimensions of the rural crisis.

The Food and Agriculture Organization (FAO) of the UN documented the experiences of 16 developing countries with the implementation of the WTO's Agreement on Agriculture and other Uruguay Round (UR) agreements affecting agriculture.[79] When markets were opened, in most cases food imports flooded in. Country after country experienced import surges that were damaging to competing domestic farming sectors. It was also typical that countries were unable to compensate for expanded imports by significantly increasing their own exports (as shown in Figure 4.1), thus leaving them in a weakened and more dependent position.

Case studies in disaster:
the 'laboratory' and the future

Mexico, thanks to its ten years of NAFTA, which came on the heels of a previous decade of liberalization under SAPs, is widely considered to be the quintessential example of the impacts of trade liberalization – the 'laboratory,' if you will.[80] Africa, on the other hand, has also experienced liberalization driven by SAPs, but as a continent is still relatively new to trade agreements, and is sometimes thought of as the next frontier for that stage of liberalization. Nevertheless, one can examine the effects of the liberalization that has already taken place in Africa.

Mexico: NAFTA, Neoliberalism, Maize and Small Farmers
For Mexico, the signing of NAFTA meant 'locking in' trade liberalization in agricultural products (tariff lowering, quota eliminating, and so on) that had begun during the previous decade as conditionality for debt relief under SAPs, and had continued as unilateral liberalization by the Mexican government in preparation for NAFTA.

On the surface it might seem that liberalization has been a resounding success for Mexico. Direct foreign investment rose from US$42 billion to US$62 billion in 1994 (under SAPs), and jumped once again to US$167 billion by 2000 (under NAFTA). Exports earnings increased similarly, from US $2.9 billion in 1980, to US$11 billion in 1994 and US$21.8 billion in 2001, though they fell off after that.[81] On the other hand, these rather spectacular figures failed to make a dent in poverty, which actually grew over the same time periods.[82]

With regard to agriculture, the process was broad in its reach over policies important to farmers, including reductions in import tariffs and quotas, steep cuts in agricultural subsidies and price supports, the privatization of government-sponsored marketing mechanisms, and the disappearance of affordable and accessible credit for peasant and family farmers. According to noted Mexican farm policy analyst Ana de Ita (2003):

> Beginning in 1989, the [Mexican] government began deepening neoliberal reforms in the countryside. State intervention diminished; credit was individualized, and the rural development bank reduced the amount of credit available for each farmer as well as the number of farmers and crops eligible for credit; subsidies fell; most of the public sector enterprises that manufactured farm inputs, or that collected, marketed or processed farm products were privatized; state services like agricultural extension, crop insurance and grain storage were privatized; the subsidies that were implicit in floor prices were eliminated, and the subsidies of numerous other public sector goods and services were slashed; protection against farm imports was reduced; and then in 1994 NAFTA came into effect, effectively functioning as the padlock on the door that prevents any return to previous policies.[83]

Though it may seem that many, if not most of these factors are 'non-trade-related' (NTR), the fact is that contemporary 'trade

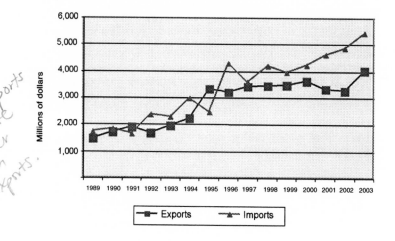

↑ imports
(a rate
higher
than
exports.

Figure 4.2 Mexico's balance of trade for farm, forest and fisheries products, before and after NAFTA (1994)

Source: De Ita, 2003.

agreements' like NAFTA, the WTO and the proposed FTAA, touch upon almost all of them, under the neoliberal pretext that they may distort the free market.[84]

While market opening by the US and Canada allowed Mexico to boost its farm exports, the opening of her own markets led to a surge of imports. After NAFTA came into effect in 1994, Mexico's modest farm trade surplus rapidly became a trade deficit. By 2003, Mexico's food trade deficit had reached US$2.7 billion (see Figure 4.2).[85]

Part of the influx of imports was made up of cheap maize from the US. For most of Mexico's family farmers, indigenous people and peasants, maize is the crop of choice and excellence. This is logical as it has formed the basis of the Mexican diet for millennia, and indeed Mexico is where indigenous people domesticated maize from its wild ancestors some 9,000 years ago. But the influx of US maize made cultivation of their own maize less and less profitable for them.

Price, million pesos

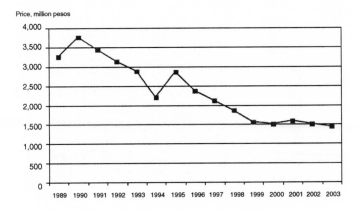

Figure 4.3 Real domestic maize prices in Mexico
Source: De Ita, 2003.

Figure 4.3 shows how the average price Mexican maize farmers receive on the domestic market has dropped by more than 50 per cent since 1990, except for a brief rise due to the massive devaluation of the peso in 1994–5.

Before NAFTA, maize represented just 2.9 per cent of Mexican farm imports, while in recent years it has fluctuated between 20 and 25 per cent of such imports.[86] Figure 4.4 shows that there was a concomitant drop in Mexican government subsidies to maize farmers, which of course is markedly different from the picture of American maize subsidies over the same time period, when subsidy levels reached as high as 47 per cent of farm income[87] (the figure for Mexico is about 13 per cent, of a much lower average income),[88] and American maize was dumped abroad at prices ranging from 13 to 33% below the cost of production.[89] How were Mexican farmers to compete?

The simplest way to conceptualize what this means is that Mexican peasant farmers found themselves with prices that were

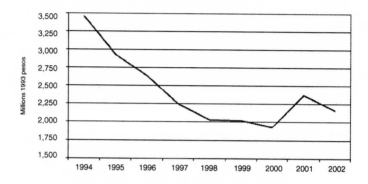

Figure 4.4 Real maize subsidies in Mexico

Source: after Wise, 2004b.

too low to turn a profit growing maize, and few buyers at any price
(as state marketing agencies were privatized and the new private
companies preferred to buy in bulk from US exporters, who were
often their close commercial associates), and little or no credit to
plant for the market anyway.

Surprisingly, given this panorama, fully half of Mexico's farmland is still planted to maize.[90] Almost three million mostly poor
peasant and indigenous farmers still grow maize, reflecting a
stubborn resistance to give up on the land, despite migration by part
of the family.[91]

How is that possible? Laura Carlsen, an analyst at the Americas
Policy Program of the Interhemispheric Resource Center who
specializes in rural Mexico, tells us that Mexican peasant farmers
themselves are subsidizing national maize production. By subsidies,
she means the wages brought or sent home from paid family labor,
from small-scale commercial activities, and from the more than
US$9 billion in annual remittances sent home by Mexicans
working in the United States:

> The remittances have a dual role. First, the money sustains
> agricultural activities that have been deemed non-viable by

the international market but that serve multiple purposes: family consumption, cultural survival, ecological conservation, supplemental income, etc. Second, by sending money home, migrants in the US seek not only to assure a decent standard of living for their Mexican families but also to maintain the *campesino* identity and community belonging that continue to define them in economic exile. Their money, whether individual or organized, subsidizes rural infrastructure, farm equipment, inputs, and labor and conserves cultural identity. The combination of these personal subsidies and subsistence tenacity account for the otherwise unaccountable growth in corn production in Mexico – despite the overwhelming 'comparative disadvantages' of a distorted international market. They reflect a deep cultural resistance to the dislocation and denial inherent in the free trade model.[92]

reasons for continuation & growing (handwritten annotation)

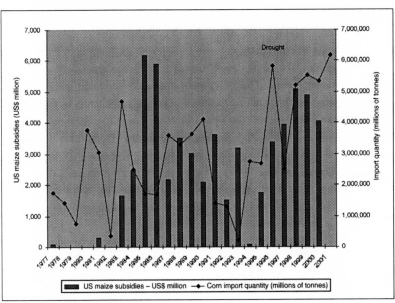

Figure 4.5   Mexican maize imports and US maize subsidies

Source: after Henriques and Patel, 2003.

In Figure 4.5 we see an apparently close relationship between Mexico's maize imports, and subsidies paid to maize farmers in the United States. Before the market opening of the late 1980s in Mexico, there was little apparent relationship. The two import spikes (1983 and 1995-96) were the product of Commodity Credit Corporation (CCC) concessional loans to Mexico, in which Mexico agreed to use this credit to import American corn, linked, in the first case at least, to US government efforts to alleviate a farm crisis at home.[93] In 1995–6 Mexican importers took on an estimated US$1.5 billion in CCC credits, with devastating impacts on Mexican maize farmers.[94] Between 1997 and 2002 the CCC provided Mexican importers with another US$1.4 billion in credits, offered on terms much more favorable than financing available in Mexico to purchase grains from Mexican farmers.[95] Export credits from the CCC are a bone of contention in the international trade debate, as they are currently excluded from WTO and NAFTA discipline, though somewhat dubious commitments have been made to eliminate them.

But we would do well to take such an apparently close relationship between subsidies and dumping at face value, as subsidy payments are made in response to low prices, and low prices lead to dumping, with or without subsidies. It appears that even in the case of maize in Mexico, the simple cancellation of US subsidies might not alleviate the cheap price of imports. According to studies summarized by Tim Wise at Tufts University, the removal of US subsidies would be unlikely to lead to more than a 4 per cent increase in maize prices, hardly enough to make a dent in the price wall facing Mexican maize producers.

On the other hand, there is a high degree of concentration in the Mexican maize market.[96] Just nine maize importing companies in Mexico accounted for half of all imports in 2001. These 'Mexican' companies included some of the biggest international players, like Archer Daniels Midland (ADM) and its Mexican partner (Maseca), Cargill, Arancia (Corn Products International), Pilgrims Pride, and

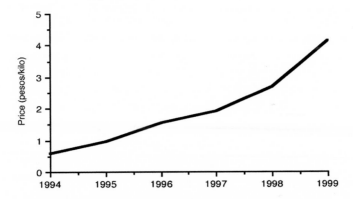

Figure 4.6 Real consumer prices for tortillas in Mexico
Source: Nadal, 2000.

MINSA, which is jointly owned by an American investment
bank.[97] At the same time, Cargill, ADM and Zen Noh control 81
per cent of maize exports from the US. With the recent
privatization of grain marketing in Mexico, Cargill, Arancia,
Maseca and MINSA have also become the principle buyers of
maize from Mexican farmers, and MINSA and Maseca dominate
the processing, distribution and retailing of tortillas – the principle
staple of the Mexican diet, which are made from maize. Perhaps
because the entire maize commodity chain is so concentrated in the
hands of so few companies, Mexican consumers have failed to
benefit from cheap imports, as shown in Figure 4.6, as the price
paid by Mexican consumers soared by more than 300 per cent in
the first five years of NAFTA.[98]

Mexico was perceived to have won a victory in the original
NAFTA negotiations because quantitative restrictions (import
quotas) and tariffs were not to be eliminated immediately, but
rather phased out over a 15-year period through a tariff rate quota
(TRQ) system. NAFTA gives the Mexican government the right
to fix monthly import quotas for maize, and to prohibit above-
quota imports or impose a tariff on them. However, the reality has

been quite different, as the Mexican government has routinely failed to exercise that right, with above quota imports often rivaling the allowed imports.[99] This is a clear example of how, in Mexico, a concentrated industry which benefits from cheap imports, has more policy clout than do millions of peasant farmers.

The tripling of maize imports since NAFTA, with as much as one-third of all maize being imported, has also brought with it the widespread contamination of native corn varieties – the genetic and cultural heritage, as we have seen, of 9,000 years of indigenous and peasant communities in Mexico. Transgenes have moved to native varieties by cross-pollination from illicit plantings of genetically engineered (GE) maize from the US, with still unknown but very worrying potential impacts.[100]

The NAFTA years have been negative for other Mexican farm products as well. Imports of soybeans, wheat, poultry and beef grew by over 500 per cent, displacing Mexican production, and breaking down vertical integration in the Mexican food and beverage processing industry.[101]

Overall, the impact of NAFTA on the rural poor in Mexico has not been positive. In ten years 1,175,000 people have been displaced from Mexican agriculture, with notable increases in malnutrition and ballooning numbers of school drop-outs.[102] The six billion *pesos* in agro-export earnings claimed by the Fox Administration under NAFTA went to just 7 per cent of Mexico's farmers. By 2003 Mexican peasants could take it no more, coming together in the *El Campo No Aguanta Más* coalition (literally, 'the countryside can't take any more of this'). January 31 saw the biggest farmer protest in Mexico City since the 1930s,[103] and in September peasant organizations manned the barricades in the street protests at the WTO ministerial.

To sum up the Mexican experiences with trade liberalization and neoliberal policies for agriculture, there have been clear winners and losers. The losers have been the vast majority of Mexico's farmers, especially the peasant and indigenous majority.

US dumping of under-priced farm products on the Mexican economy has severely undercut their ability to make a living. Only by tearing apart family units through migration to generate remittances have they able cling to the land at all.

On the other hand, the clear winners have been American agribusiness companies and their Mexican partners and subsidiaries. According to Laura Carlsen:

(X) including govts

> [They] have grown by leaps and bounds under the auspices of the free trade model. As international traders with both export and import activities, many receive a triple subsidy under NAFTA: (1) as exporters of below-cost US farm products, (2) as recipients of direct export subsidies, and (3) as Mexican importers. They also get Mexican subsidies; for example, Cargill receives the lion's share of subsidies in the state of Sinaloa – Mexico's most heavily subsidized agricultural state. Couple that with the added advantage of wiping competition off the map through below-cost prices and the deal is complete.

Other relative winners include the 7 per cent of Mexican farmers able to compete in the export market.

WTO-exempt export credits seem to have had a role in generating this situation, though there is evidence to suggest that even the full elimination of domestic subsidies in the US would have little or no effect on the critical problem of dumping, which seems to result far more from the absence of price supports, the lack of supply management, and the concentrated nature of commodity markets in which an ever-smaller number of companies controls an ever-larger market share.

Africa: liberalization and import dependency

Liberalization in most African countries, generally mandated by SAPs, has typically included market opening, reduced credit for small farmers, and the contraction or privatization of state grain marketing enterprises which, while riddled with problems,

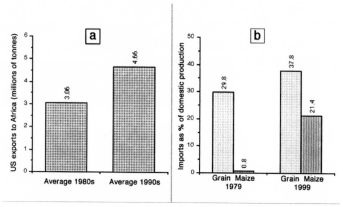

**Figure 4.7 Average annual US grain exports to Africa in the 1980s
and 1990s (a), and African total grain and maize imports
(quantity) as a percentage of African domestic grain and maize
production in 1979 versus 1999 (b)**

Source: FAOSTAT.

previously offered small farmers some guarantee of minimum prices
and access to national markets. Market opening has often led to
surges in imports, and the consequent hemorrhaging of scarce
foreign exchange and severe balance of payments problems. In a
number of cases this has pushed governments into policy reversals.[104]

US grain exports to Africa have grown during the decades of
SAPs, privatization and, to the extent that it has already occurred,
WTO-led market opening. As American grain exports to Africa
have grown, so has the proportion of grain imported by African
countries compared to their own domestic production, particularly
in the case of maize. Figure 4.7a shows the growth in US grain
exports to Africa from the 1980s to the 1990s. Figure 4.7b shows
how imported grain as a percentage of domestic production has
grown from some 30 per cent to about 38 per cent in twenty years,
while imported maize grew from less than 1 per cent of domestic
production to more than 21 per cent, evidencing a tendency
toward growing dependency on imports.

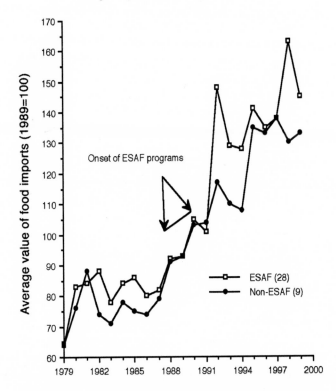

Figure 4.8 Average per country value of food imports (index year, 1989=100) in Sub-Saharan Africa for 28 countries with Enhanced Structural Adjustment (ESAF) programs and 9 without, 1979–99

Sources: IMF, 1999b (list of countries); FAOSTAT (value of imports).

Wheat imports in Africa have been typical of this trend, increasing by 35 per cent between 1996 and 2000, while the total value of these ever-cheaper imports actually fell by 13 per cent, on average. In Burkina Faso, for example, imports were up by 84 per cent, although the value increase was only 16 per cent. This dumping of basic foodstuffs caused French-speaking West Africa to invest heavily in cotton production as an alternative to food production. West Africa has an advantage over competitors because production costs in that area are the lowest in the world, but then the price of cotton collapsed. The collapse was not due as much to heavy American, European and Chinese subsidies, which were not new, but to the end of supply management by the US in 1996. As a result, West Africa lost some US$200 million a year between 1997 and 2001.[105]

Beginning in 1987, the International Monetary Fund placed a number of countries in Sub-Saharan Africa under 'Enhanced Structural Adjustment' (ESAF) programs.[106] This involved debt relief under concessional terms in exchange for intensifying SAP provisions. In Figure 4.8 we observe that increased imports, as a consequence of the greater market opening forced on them, was a feature of these countries. As we saw in the Mexican case, greater food imports have a tendency to make it difficult for national and especially smaller and poorer farmers to compete, as they tend to depress crop prices.[107]

In sum, liberalization in Africa has opened markets to a flood of imports, and eliminated public sector institutions that fulfilled vital functions for small farmers, though they also suffered from internal and external political and economic weaknesses. These weaknesses should have been corrected instead of just closing up shop. The combined result has been a net loss of markets for smaller, poorer farmers in more remote areas. Just as in Mexico, rising costs and increasing uncertainty of daily life have led farmers to diversify their economic activity away from their own farms, to the detriment of their own productivity, production and family life. Export crop production was touted as a means of raising farmer incomes, but has been thwarted by geographical and social inequities that have combined with glutted world markets. Market opening in the context of SAPs and the WTO has weakened the relative competitive ability of African countries, while forcing their farmers into an impossible competition with a flood of cheap food imports from abroad.[108] Overall, agricultural liberalization in Africa has shown similar trends to those observed in Mexico, as imports capture an increasingly large share of domestic markets, to the detriment of local producers.

5

Alternatives for a Different Agriculture and Food System

Trade liberalization through the WTO and other agreements is part of a larger process that is taking us farther away from the kind of food and agriculture system most people might wish, one which:

- provides every one of us with adequate, affordable, healthy, tasty, and culturally appropriate food;

- offers rural peoples in each of our countries the opportunity for a life with dignity, in which they earn a living wage for their labor and have the opportunity to remain in rural areas if they prefer not to migrate to cities;

- contributes to broad-based, inclusive economic development at the local, regional and national level;

- conserves rural environments and landscapes, and rural-based cultural and culinary traditions, based on the sustainable long-term management of productive natural resources (soils, water, genetic resources and other biodiversity) by rural peoples themselves.

The majorities of most countries are increasingly faced with food choices that are unhealthy and expensive, taste bad, and run counter to local and national culinary traditions. Rural peoples are more and more being forced by economic necessity to abandon the land and seek their fortune in peri-urban slums and shanty towns, or join the global migrant stream. Rural economies are in a state of economic collapse, from Iowa to Africa, and agriculture contributes ever less to local, regional and national economic development. Rural environments are being rapidly degraded, their soils compacted, eroded, poisoned with pesticides, and stripped of biodiversity.

Policy options

To move back toward something more like what we want, we need concrete policy options that operationalize the ideals expressed in the alternative paradigms of multifunctionality and food sovereignty (see **People's Food Sovereignty Statement** on p. 126). Toward that end, a good number of mostly complementary, commonsense proposals have been made. They are mostly complementary in the broad sense, because they overlie serious differences of opinion over whether the proper forum to achieve them is in the WTO and other trade agreements, or in some other set of already existing and/or to-be-created venues. A remarkably broad global coalition of groups is coalescing around some or all of these options.[109] They include organizations of family farmers, peasants, indigenous people, trade unions, consumers, policy institutes, academics and others. What follows are brief summaries of the most salient proposals.

Market access and protection: stop dumping and pay fair prices
When poorer countries are obliged to give more foreign access to their domestic markets than richer countries provide for them, most observers consider the system unbalanced and unjust. Once they open their markets they become susceptible to dumping. Most actors seem to agree, at least rhetorically, that ending dumping

should be a goal of international negotiations in agriculture. Several steps can be taken to make this a reality.[110]

First, we need to eliminate visible and hidden export subsidies as quickly as possible, though that is not as easy as it sounds. In theory this is agreed upon even by governments in the WTO, while in practice there are a myriad of ways these subsidies are disguised and hidden (see **How the WTO Rules Agriculture**, p. 81). A possibly simpler approach would be to ban international trade in farm products at prices below the cost of production (costs plus a return to farm families sufficient for a living wage). This will require the creation of clear guidelines for full-cost accounting of commodity production. Some international agency will have to develop a methodology and publish the results, establishing a baseline for costs of production in each exporting country to be used to determine whether dumping is taking place. Such a methodology should take into account all input and general subsidies, as well as indirect subsidies such as the subsidized cost of feed grains for meat and dairy products.

Second, because voluntary compliance is unlikely, all countries must be permitted a broad range of options to protect themselves from dumping. For example, all countries should be allowed to impose countervailing duties or take other protective measures – like import quotas or outright bans – if agricultural exports from other countries are being dumped at below the costs of production. Furthermore, to protect food security and family farmer/peasant livelihoods, countries should be able to protect any key food crops without having to prove dumping is taking place.

Third, experience tells us that it is hard, nevertheless, for politically weaker countries to impose countervailing duties to protect themselves from the dumping practices of powerful countries. The world trading system is based on profound asymmetries of political and economic power. To effectively end dumping will require complementary policies inside the United States, the European Union, and other major agro-exporters. These must be policies to ensure that export prices capture the full cost of production, including the cost of marketing and a reasonable profit. In the United States, where domestic and world prices are pretty much the same, this could be done by reestablishing a floor price for farm products, as called for by the National Family Farm Coalition (see **Food from Family Farms Act: a Proposal**, p. 107). Support prices are minimum prices for agricultural products, set by the government.

This would function much as a minimum or living wage law, forcing corporations that want to buy commodities from farmers to at least match the floor price offered by government. If this price is set at least at the cost of production plus a fair profit, this would ensure that commodities are not placed on the market at dumping prices. A significant side benefit for the US farmers would be to guarantee them fair prices for what they produce, something that they have not been able to achieve in decades.

Supply management: regulate overproduction

The 1996 Freedom to Farm Act in the US eliminated price floors (minimum prices) and impeded the implementation of supply management land set-asides and grain reserves. The effect was to let prices drop and force farmers to boost production to compensate, planting fencerow to fencerow, the additional production feeding the downward spiral of prices. And as prices dropped, subsidies rose in response.[111]

Perpetual global overproduction is a mutually reinforcing, downward spiral for the world's farmers, as they struggle to produce more and more to compensate for lower and lower prices, matched against the ever-higher production costs of the industrial farming model. A relatively small number of agro-export powers, led by the US and the EU, are responsible for most of the overproduction. It is notable that the major family farm coalitions in both the US (the National Family Farm Coalition) and Europe (European Farmers Coordination) – both are members of Via Campesina – call for a return to supply management policies and price supports, not just on a national level, but internationally as well (see **Where European and American Family Farmers Stand**, p.97 and **Where Peasant and Family Farmer Organizations Stand**, p. 102).

Clearly, regulating production runs counter to market fundamentalism. Yet we are a far cry from the Adam Smith vision of free markets when we have such high levels of market concentration, which economists agree severely distort market signals. Farm organizations want to get out of the downward spiral they find themselves in, and are crying out for sensible regulation.

To do this requires two steps.[112] The first is to reinstate improved production-limiting policies for key crops in the US and the EU. The only proven way to reduce production in the North is to take land out of production and reinstitute management of surpluses – for the public good – and prices. There must be some sort of mechanism which keeps agribusiness from seizing effective, even if indirect, control of the surpluses, and which involves both government and family farm representatives in planning and decision making. Subsidized farmer-owned reserves will most likely need to be a central part of the system, as well as a return to greater use of the 'non-recourse loan' in the US. This allows farmers to take excess supply off the market in times of abundance, and place it back on the market in times of shortage. According to George Naylor:

> The non-recourse loan is the most important social invention of the twentieth century for agriculture. It does in fact set a floor price, and only in isolated regions where crops are very bountiful would prices go below loan. If that occurs and the farmer doesn't get the grain sold, he/she can forfeit the grain to the reserve, which becomes a valuable asset for food security and will only be sold back on the market when an unforeseen crop shortfall drives up the price. Other than the cost of the money tied up in this and the cost of storage, the government might actually make a profit on it, so

government outlays [wouldn't] go up in response to falling prices. With the grain forfeiture, the outlay is for an investment, not simply an income transfer like the other direct and counter-cyclical payments.[113]

Good models to learn from – not copy – exist, one of them being the Canadian Wheat Board. Added benefits include encouraging soil conservation, the ability to redirect domestic supports away from corporate farms and toward family farmers, improving incomes for family farmers, and even reducing subsidies, since many are the result of low prices. This is an area in need of further study.

Ray *et al.* ran simulations for an alternative US policy scenario based on a combination of (1) acreage diversion through short-term acreage set-asides and longer-term acreage reserves, both of which take land out of production; (2) a farmer-owned food security reserve; and (3) price supports.[114] They found that such a program, despite having its own costs, would lead to a net reduction of $10–12 billion per year in US farm subsidies – a massive savings for taxpayers – though it would only boost the crop prices farmers receive by a moderate amount. But the critical conclusion from their analysis is that by taking a step back from 'free' markets, we can greatly reduce the cost to taxpayers of subsidies and provide a basis for greater family farmer competitiveness.

The second required step is to correct structural oversupply at the global level with international supply management agreements. Farmer organizations and others call for close study of the old commodity agreements under the United Nations Conference on Trade and Development (UNCTAD), which were the pre-Uruguay Round mainstay of international trade regulation. While the International Coffee Agreement, for example, was riddled with problems, coffee farmers were incomparably better protected before its collapse than they are now. Nevertheless, the collapse of many of these agreements was due not so much to their internal weaknesses, but to the withdrawal of the political support of developed countries.[115] The study of these agreements and how to improve them must be taken up urgently.[116]

Market concentration: a return to anti-trust enforcement?

Reducing the market concentration of agribusiness conglomerates may well need to be the first step. Note that the Ray *et al.* study found that a lot of taxpayer money could be saved with supply management, but that farmer prices would nevertheless remain low. That may be because they left the concentrated structure of agriculture markets intact in their alternative scenario.

Not only is the ability of large conglomerates to fix prices a key driving force behind low farm prices *and* high consumer prices, but their size gives them the political leverage to 'bend' government policy makers and trade negotiators to their will. Without weakening their grip on markets and political power, few of the changes proposed in this book would be possible.[117]

Unfortunately the WTO negotiations on 'competition policy' are focused on breaking the power of state enterprises to intervene in prices, rather than on the power of TNCs to collude to fix prices. These are the very state enterprises that once provided a floor price to peasant producers in the Third World, and that have been cut back or privatized outright by structural adjustment and trade agreements. Farmers need such bodies – albeit less corrupt ones than their defunct predecessors – so the WTO approach is completely wrong-headed. What is needed is a global competition policy directed at the main purveyors of damaging anti-competitive practices: agribusiness oligopolies. This is not to say that that the WTO would be the correct venue for such a policy, rather it is to say that we urgently need one.

The place to begin is with active enforcement and application of existing anti-trust and anti-monopoly legislation in the US, the EU, and in the many countries that have similar laws on their books. Once again, this is not as easy at it sounds. While the US is widely seen as a model country for anti-trust legislation, enforcement has been progressively weaker in recent decades. Statistics reported by Sofia Murphy of the Institute for Agricultural Trade Policy (IATP) show that from October 1994 to September 1996, the US Department of Agriculture's Grain Inspection and Packers and Stockyards Administration (GIPSA) received over 2,000 complaints of anti-trust violations of GIPSA rules. GIPSA estimated that 800 of the complaints pointed to a clear violation of the law, yet chronic funding, staffing and training shortages meant that only 84 cases were investigated. Of these, only three were put forward for enforcement action.[118]

Such laws are only enforced as the result of mass movements. The great trust busting of the late 1800s and early 1900s was driven by a mass movement of American farmers, and many of the big trusts of the time (railroads, meat-packing, petroleum, sugar, tobacco) were busted.[119] Once again, in today's world, we see farmer organizations taking the lead in calling for the regulation of the conglomerates that they feel are strangling them. This time we also need the international review of multinational mergers and acquisitions as part of our multilateral machinery, so as to ensure that developing countries' food needs are not sacrificed to multinationals' interest in profits. Perhaps a global anti-monopoly agency is in order.

Public sector budgets: 'subsidy' is not a bad word

We need to remember the distinction made by Via Campesina and other farm groups between inappropriate and wasteful subsidies and necessary, legitimate public services and rural and economic development strategies. Unfortunately they have all been tarred with the same brush: 'subsidies are bad.'

Farmer organizations worldwide insist that farmers need many things from public sector budgets, including credit, marketing assistance, supply management, price regulation, research, extension, education, roads, infrastructure, access to productive resources, environmental protection, pesticide regulation, anti-trust enforce-

ment ... the list goes on. It is safe to say that no country currently
considered 'developed' got that way without government supports
for agriculture, and no family or peasant farmer anywhere in the
world who is 'well-off' does not benefit in some way from such
supports. It is urgent that we stop labeling 'subsidies' as a bad word.
The issue is what kind of subsidies, for what, and given to whom.
This must be the subject of national dialog and society-wide
priority setting in each country, as each country is different. The
key at the international level is to strictly and effectively ban all
direct and indirect, open and hidden subsidies that support or
boost overproduction and/or exports, but clearly and unam-
biguously to permit other, positive kinds of subsidies and public
sector budgets.[120]

Intellectual property rights and other WTO issues that impinge on agriculture

While this book has focused on the agricultural trade and subsidy
issues contained in the Agreement on Agriculture framework, that
should in no way suggest that there are not many other aspects of
the WTO and other trade agreements that impinge upon food,
agriculture, and the livelihoods of rural peoples. Trade agreement
clauses on competition, investment, government procurement and
many other areas of life all also have critical impacts. But perhaps
the most notable aspect that is beyond the general purview of this
report, is that of intellectual property rights (IPRs) and patents on
life, which in WTO parlance is contained in the TRIPS (Trade-
Related Aspects of Intellectual Property Rights) negotiations. This
is where the controversies over biopiracy (when TNCs patent
traditional crop varieties) and genetically engineered crops and
livestock come in. Most of the civil society actors campaigning on
trade issues have strong positions against patents on life and in favor
of the right of nations to use the precautionary principle when it
comes to GE organisms and foods.[121]

Venues and forums: WTO out of food and agriculture?

As alluded to above, there is considerable discussion as to whether or not any of these alternatives can be obtained in the context of WTO or other trade agreement negotiations. Noted globalization theorist Walden Bello has argued convincingly that the WTO is not the venue in which to regulate corporate activity, or to achieve anything other than trade liberalization of an asymmetric, pro-US/EU variety.[122] La Via Campesina has made 'WTO out of food and agriculture' its rallying cry, backed by family farm and peasant organizations worldwide. The WTO and other trade liberalization agreements are by nature designed from the ground up to favor the removal of barriers to trade, rather than its regulation in the public interest, and the non-transparent, anti-democratic, superpower-dominated mechanisms they use are unlikely to make anything else possible.[123] Bello and others suggest a strategy of reducing the purview of the WTO, while simultaneously trying to revive certain instruments of the in-theory more democratic United Nations system, like UNCTAD, the International Labor Organization (ILO) and, in this case, the FAO.[124] La Via Campesina and allied organizations and movements call for a new dialog on the future of food and agriculture centered on the FAO, UNCTAD and the ILO (see **Where Peasant and Family Farmer Organizations Stand**, p. 102).

Parallel anti-WTO movements of people from other sectors, who are also negatively affected by WTO policies in areas like industry and services,[125] provide us with legitimate arguments that the world might be a better place if the WTO ceased to existed altogether. Thus the argument of La Via Campesina is really, 'WTO out of *at least* food and agriculture.'

At the national level, key venues for policy change include the Farm Bill process in the US, the CAP reform process in the EU, and national farm policy setting mechanisms in all countries. In the US, the National Family Farm Coalition has proposed an alternative Farm Bill that would meet the objectives outlined above (see **Food**

from **Family Farms Act: a Proposal** , p. 107),[126] and in the EU the
European Farmers Coordination has proposed such an alternative
CAP reform (see **For a Legitimate, Sustainable and Supportive CAP**
on p. 116).[127]

Coalition building

As Tim Wise has said,[128] these measures face many obstacles, most
notably the concerted opposition of the powerful corporations –
and their government allies – that currently benefit most from the
global trading system in agriculture. Yet these proposals also offer a
number of advantages that make them at least as plausible as the
notion that we could really eliminate Northern farm subsidies.

First of all, they make natural allies of farmer and peasant groups
around the world, North and South, East and West, as has been
amply demonstrated by Via Campesina. The proposals also lay the
initial groundwork for broader coalitions and alliances within
national and global civil society. Such alliances, in favor of a better
food and agriculture system, might unite sectors as diverse as family
farmers, peasants, indigenous peoples, farm workers, small-scale
fisherfolk, pastoralists, consumers, environmentalists, human rights
advocates and religious groups, to name a few.

These proposals could also provide a common ground for many
Third World and G10 governments, were it possible to wean them
from agribusiness and agro-export influences. They infringe less on
national sovereignty, allowing countries to choose the measures
they prefer for the food and farming systems they want, as long as
such policies do not lead to export dumping, and they could be a lot
cheaper in terms of taxpayer dollars spent on farm subsidies, with
much better outcomes for most of society.

Conclusion:
Another Food System is Possible

We can do it. Why must we put up with a global food system that ruins rural economies worldwide, drives family and peasant farmers off the land in droves, and into slums, ghettos and international migrant streams? That kills farmers. That imposes a kind of agriculture that destroys the soil, contaminates ground water, eliminates trees from rural areas, creates pests that are resistant to pesticides, and puts the future productivity of agriculture in doubt? A food system that gives us expensive, unhealthy and foul-tasting food, where we often pay more for packaging and long-distance shipping than we do for the food itself? Food that is laden with sugar, salt, fat, starch, carcinogenic colors and preservatives, pesticide residues and genetically modified organisms, and that may well be driving global epidemics of obesity for some (and hunger for others) heart disease, diabetes and cancer? A food system that bloats the coffers of unaccountable corporations, corrupts governments and kills farmers and consumers while wrecking the environment?

I say enough is enough. Or *'Basta!'* as the Zapatistas said in Chiapas, Mexico. Those of us who are harmed by the system are the majority. We are, in fact, the *vast* majority of people around the world, in the North, South, East and West. Those who benefit are few: the major shareholders of a few corporations, and corrupted officials. I believe that we can all follow the lead of La Vía Campesina, and take a platform like People's Food Sovereignty (see

p. 126) to build a broad coalition at the local, national and global levels. A coalition that mobilizes the power of our numbers, to achieve real change.

Food *is* different. It is not a typical commodity because it affects so many people – and the environment – in such intimate ways. Food has the power to move us to action. Food is both personal (it affects our bodies) and political (it affects the world), and by working on food issues, in the personal interest of each one of us, we can build political power.

We can have a food system that gives all of us healthy, tasty, affordable and culturally appropriate food. That helps human beings – peasants, family farmers, indigenous people, and others – stay in rural areas, and that protects rural environments and ecosystems. In Chapter 5 we saw examples of simple, common-sense policy instruments that in many cases are based on enforcing laws that already exist (like anti-trust measures) or on recovering improved versions of past policies (such as supply management), and thus are not so far out of reach. The first step is to reverse runaway trade liberalization, whether it comes via the WTO, or via regional or bilateral trade agreements, and to give every people and nation the right to design their own food and agriculture policies, policies that are pro-family farmer, pro-peasant, pro-environment and pro-consumer, as long as those policies do not hurt third parties via dumping or excessive exports.

Is this really too much to ask? – A food system that is good for people and the environment, and that is possible, rather than one that hurts all of us? Let us build the grand coalition, and the movement that it will take to make what is possible and desirable into a reality. Starting now.

WTO Kills Farmers!
WTO and Other Free Trade Agreements Out of
Food and Agriculture!
Another World *is* Possible!

very manifesto-esque, rallying support for VC?!

SPECIAL TOPICS

How the WTO Rules Agriculture[129]

The Three Pillars of the AoA

The first version of the Agreement on Agriculture (AoA) of the Uruguay Round of the General Agreement on Tariffs and Trade (GATT) took effect with the creation of the WTO on 1 January 1995. Under this agreement, countries were to reduce export subsidies and domestic supports, while lowering import barriers (increasing market access). In the WTO, the negotiations on agricultural trade are said to rest on three 'pillars:'

- **Market access.** Under the initial AoA, all member countries were required to eliminate quantitative restrictions (import quotas) and non-tariff barriers, and replace these with tariffs. Members also had to reduce their tariff levels: by 36 per cent over six years (1995–2000) for developed countries, and by 24 per cent over ten years (1995–2004) for developing countries. The poorest countries ('least-developed countries,' or LDCs) did not have to reduce their tariffs, but nevertheless committed to not raising them either. Under a more recent framework agreed to in 2004, a commitment was made to cut higher tariffs more than lower tariffs. While this seems reasonable at face value, it actually discriminates heavily against poorer countries. While wealthier countries can support farmers in numerous ways that require significant levels of spending, poorer countries cannot afford the outlays. Virtually the only way they can support their farmers is through tariffs or other restrictions on imports that limit dumping in their home markets and help keep domestic crop prices up. An article in the *New York Times* (1 August 2004), makes this clear: 'The United States was pleased that negotiators agreed that the highest tariffs should be cut the most, a move that would mean a greater opening for American agricultural products in the developing world. "We feel this is a win-win for the United States, the WTO, exporters, consumers, developed and developing countries alike," said an American trade official who asked for anonymity.'

Market access is at once the 'Holy Grail,' or bait held out to Southern countries – access, in their case, to US and EU markets – and the real goal of the trade superpowers in ongoing negotiations, which is access to poor country markets for US and EU exports. The former is typically held closely as a bargaining chip by the US and EU, to be doled out bit by bit in each round of negotiations in exchange for yet wider opening of Southern markets. When one considers that agricultural exports are typically equivalent to less than 10 per cent of agricultural value-added in LDCs, the bargain with the devil that is on offer becomes clear. 'Give us more market access for dumping into your 90 per cent (the domestic food market for which the vast majority of small farmers produce), and we'll give you more of a chance for your 10 per cent in our markets (the tiny elite of large agro-exporters).' Unfortunately for family and peasant farmers the world over (responsible for producing the 90 per cent), their governments are usually beholden to small but immensely powerful agro-export elites. Thus have most Third World governments bitten hard on the market access bait.

- **Export subsidies.** This is the 'Red Box' that should eventually be prohibited. Direct export subsidies were subject to reductions by 36 per cent in value and 21 per cent in volume from 1986–8 average amounts for developed countries, and by 24 per cent in value and 14 per cent in volume for developing countries over ten years.

- **Domestic support.** The stated rationale for lowering domestic supports was to reduce subsidies that might end up paying, one way or another, for production destined for export. However, separating the multiple effects of complex support schemes is a difficult task, as many kinds of payments can directly or indirectly boost production, and excess production may spill over as cut-rate products placed in export markets – dumping – or may crowd out imports from competing in the home market, reducing market access for others. To deal with this complexity, domestic support measures have been divided into three categories, called 'boxes.' The Amber Box refers to measures that are trade-distorting and can lead to increased production, such as input subsidies. The Blue Box refers to programs that do the opposite, such as direct payments to farmers for programs to limit production. And the Green Box includes measures that are assumed to have no effect on production, such as public sector financing of research, or assistance for marketing crops. Different color boxes are subject to different degrees of what is called 'discipline' (reduction), or lack thereof. This is all explained in more detail below. However, the contents of the boxes are not always what they seem, and, there are a number of other kinds of domestic supports that fall outside the boxes, leading at least one analyst to propose additional boxes, as discussed below.

It should be clear that countries in the South have been subjected to virtually the same requirement to liberalize their agricultural sectors as the Northern countries – despite pre-existing asymmetries – the principle concession being somewhat lower rates of reduction over slightly longer time periods. The poorest countries do not have to reduce their tariffs or subsidies, but they cannot raise them either, something they might well need to do if they were ever to switch

assumes *an equal playing field to start*

development tracks. Obviously the two biggest spenders on domestic support are the US and the EU. The boxes, which permit virtually unlimited spending on certain categories of domestic support, mean little or nothing to most developing countries, who lack the financial wherewithal to provide significant domestic support programs. However, the boxes are playing a critical role in the ongoing negotiations and conflicts, as they are widely perceived to be the mechanisms by which the North 'hides' its subsidies, leading to a global backlash – most evident in Seattle and Cancún – against what is widely perceived as US and EU hypocrisy and doublespeak.

The 'hide the subsidy' shell game

The three 'boxes' to which domestic supports are assigned, constitute in many ways a global shell game in which the EU and the US repeatedly claim to the rest of the world to have made massive reductions in subsidies, when in fact they have been (not so) surreptitiously taken from a prohibited or limited box and 'hidden' in an unlimited box.

Amber Box: 'Trade-distorting' subsidies (must be reduced, but not eliminated)

Subsidies in the Amber Box are calculated under the Aggregate Measure of Support (AMS) and are subject to reduction. These are programs and policies that are recognized as 'distorting' to patterns of trade, and are comprised of payments to farmers and other domestic supports that are 'coupled' to production (the more you produce, the more you get). These include 'product-specific' subsidies such as guaranteed prices (the 'loan deficiency payment' in the US or the 'intervention price' in the EU), and 'non-product-specific subsidies' on inputs or investments. The original requirement was for developed countries to cut Amber Box supports by 20 per cent over five years, and for the developing countries to cut them by 13.3 per cent over nine years (from a 1986–88 baseline, when payments were unusually high in the US and EU.) Developed countries are allowed to keep a total of Amber Box support that is equivalent to up to 5 per cent of total agricultural production, plus an additional 5 per cent of value on a per crop basis. Developing countries are given 10 per cent for each. LDCs are exempted from these reduction commitments; however, they have also committed not to raise their total level of support beyond the '*de minimis* level' (equal to 10 per cent of the total value of production of a 'specific product,' or 10 per cent of total agricultural production for 'non-specific' supports, for developing countries, and 5 per cent for developed countries).

Blue Box: Unlimited payments to limit production

Countries with production-limiting programs can fund them with unlimited levels of support. The US abandoned such programs in 1996, though they still exist to some extent in other developed countries. The problem comes when countries disguise other kinds of subsidies and supports as Blue Box measures, as in July 2004 when the US tried to modify the Blue Box, and thus include 'direct payments unrelated to current production,' and of course unrelated to limiting production, a proposal that was soundly rejected at the time by the G10 countries, but eventually made its way into the official negotiating framework. However, a serious effort by the major agro-exporting countries to truly limit their production, starting with the US and the EU, would be roundly welcomed by the rest of the world.

Green Box: The best shell for hiding subsidies?

This is where one finds some 70 per cent of total US and 25 per cent of EU domestic supports. These 'de-coupled' supports and payments in theory do not have major effects on patterns and flows of trade, and thus unlimited amounts are permitted. Under the Green Box governments can provide supports for, among other purposes, environmentally sound practices, pest and crop disease management, infrastructure, food storage against famine, income insurance, emergency programs, and so-called 'decoupled payments,' which are direct payments that are not linked to production levels. These decoupled payments are still direct payments to farmers that support their incomes. The effect of these payments is still to shield their recipients (large producers in developed countries) from downswings in crop prices, and means that they need not receive crop prices above the cost of production in order to stay in business. The United States has long 'hid' a big part of its subsidies here, and ostensibly the June 2003 reform of the EU's Common Agricultural Policy (CAP) was designed to eliminate the export subsidies that were causing major friction with the US, the Cairn's group, and everybody else, and replace them with an equal amount of 'decoupled' payments, thus not affecting the overall size of the EU subsidies at all. By doing so, the EU came into line with the US Farm Bill, claiming, just as the US does, that the bulk of its payments are non-trade-distorting and thus permissible.

When the EU switched over the to the American system of decoupled payments, it eliminated the need to pay for price supports or subsidize exports. Essentially, the EU now allows internal prices to fall down to world price levels, and compensates farmers for lost income with decoupled payments. Export subsidies are then no longer needed to make European exports competitive, because they are essentially being produced now at 'dumping' prices on the EU domestic market. Thus does dumping go on without significant 'discipline' from the WTO.

The missing boxes

As if the combination of Amber, Blue and Green boxes did not offer rich nations enough ways to secure an advantage over poor countries in the global market for agricultural goods, there are all kinds of other 'support' to agribusiness enterprises in the these countries that are unavailable or impossible in poor countries. If it were possible – and it is difficult – to accurately add up all the support in the first three boxes, we would then have to estimate and add on the even harder to calculate additional supports that French analyst Jacques Berthelot calls, with tongue in cheek, the Gold, Brown, Purple and White boxes.[130] These, plus concrete production costs, would then give us an implicit real total production cost which with to compare the prices at which US and EU products reach world markets, thus giving the ability to estimate the true amount of dumping going on. From the Betholet perspective, there is Amber, Blue and Green box dumping, and then there is also Gold, Brown, Purple and White box dumping.

The Gold Box: 'living in the First World'

By the simple virtue of being based in a wealthy country, agri-businesses benefit from all kinds of hidden subsidies, especially in the broad sense of the non-specific and non-agricultural subsidies which underlie the higher competitiveness of their products relative to poor countries. In reality, there is a continuum from non-specific agricultural subsidies to non-agricultural general subsidies which apply to all sectors, and it would be arbitrary to separate specific support for agricultural research, education, extension, and infra-structure from general support for all research, education, social security, and infrastructure, and everything else that lowers trans-actions costs of all kinds under higher levels of economic development (like enforcement of contracts, for instance).

Brown Box: social dumping

All of the major agro-export countries practice what might be called 'social dumping,' whether they are 'developed' country exporters like the US, EU, Canada and Australia, or 'developing' country export powers like Brazil, China, South Africa and Chile. Social dumping refers to the externalization of the social costs of low-cost mass production, costs to all of society that arise from paying farm workers below living wages, forcing their children to join them in the fields, denying them social security, and the costs of land concentration and growing landlessness, etc.

Purple Box: environmental dumping

American agribusinesses pay three to four times less for their petroleum than most of the rest of the world, at the cost of petroleum exploration by, and wars on behalf of, American oil companies, that despoil big chunks of the world's environment. The industrialized farming systems of the big agro-exporters, both North and South, generate massive externalities not calculated in their production costs such as soil erosion, compaction and salinization, groundwater contamination with chemical pesticides and fertilizers, and loss of biodiversity.

White Box: monetary dumping

A country whose currency is the universal standard (the US today, perhaps the EU in the near future) has the unique privilege of being able to borrow and reimburse its foreign debts in its own currency, without being penalized by devaluation, thus reinforcing the competitiveness of its products. At the same time it can go on importing products without being penalized by dollar (or in the future, Euro) depreciation, since most commodities and many industrial products are routinely traded in dollars. On the other hand, poorer countries suffer from what might be called a 'reverse White Box effect,' in the sense that their domestic currency is not very convertible, so they have to maintain very high real interest rates in order to attract capital flows and limit capital outflows, making investment in agricultural production by their farmers more expensive.

Government Negotiating Blocs[131]

For years global negotiations on agricultural trade have been marked by coalitions of countries that negotiate to a greater or lesser extent as blocs. Prior to Cancún, major blocs included the sometimes together and often split US and EU, the Cairns group, and the 'Group of 77 plus China,' or 'Like Minded' nations, the inheritors of the mantle of the defunct non-aligned movement. But at the 1993 WTO summit in Cancún major shifts occurred and new alliances emerged, while older ones faded. The collapse of the Cancún Ministerial is widely attributed to a combination of astute coalition and bloc-building by the Third World and other nations, to the now obvious hypocrisy of the US and EU positions, and to the farmer/peasant movements protesting in the streets. The positions of both the government coalitions and the civil society protestors must be understood if one is to grasp fully what is at stake in these ongoing negotiations. Here we consider the new configuration of government blocs, most of which have been christened with 'G names' (G10, G20, G90, etcetera).

only farmers?

EU and USA

The EU and the US are widely known for what is perceived as hypocritical rhetoric on agricultural trade and subsidies, for fighting with each over access to each other's markets (using proxy issues like genetic engineering or beef with hormones), and, when push comes to shove, for putting aside their differences and closing ranks against the Third World by agreeing on common positions (this happened at the Seattle, Doha, Cancún and Hong Kong trade summits). Both trade superpowers profess adherence to neoliberal free trade ideology (especially the US), yet both constantly seek ways to push extreme trade liberalization and free market practices on others while heavily intervening in the 'market' to their own advantage by conserving heavy subsidies at home and tariff and non-tariff (i.e. phytosanitary) barriers to protect their own markets. Both have increasingly similar subsidy and support systems that disproportionately go to larger, wealthier farmers and agribusiness, and enforce (this is more recent for the EU) low price policies that drive their own family farmers into bankruptcy while fueling the export dumping of commodities in Third World markets. The EU has made more rhetorical reference to conserving rural livelihoods and landscapes at home, though in practice its Common Agricultural Policy (CAP) has been no less damaging to family farmers than the US Farm Bill. These superpowers have long defended their own use of domestic supports, but are increasingly willing to trade them away in exchange for greater and greater access by their corporations (Cargill, ADM, Monsanto, Nestlé, Unilever, Parmalat and the others) to Third World markets. Prior to Cancún the US masterfully used the Cairns group (see below) countries to deflect criticism to toward the EU, while hiding its own subsidies in permitted Green Box categories. Since the EU reformed the CAP in 1993 to more closely resemble the US system, this has become more difficult. Periodically the US and the EU make what appear to be major concessions in exchange for further liberalization by the rest of the world. Examples might include the EU 'giving up' export subsidies in the 2003 CAP reform – but replacing them with Green Box supports – and the US agreeing to a further '20% cut in domestic supports' in 2004, while pushing for an expanded Blue Box in which to hide their replacements (see **How the WTO Rules Agriculture**, p. 81).

Cairns Group

This powerful pre-Cancún negotiating bloc was made up of Australia, Argentina, Bolivia, Brazil, Canada, Chile, Colombia, Costa Rica, Fiji, Guatemala, Indonesia, Malaysia, New Zealand, Paraguay, Philippines, Thailand, South Africa and Uruguay. While putatively led by Australia, Cairns was often in the position of 'doing the dirty work for the United States,' attacking other Third World countries and the EU for protectionist positions and subsidies. They took the position that all forms of public intervention and subsidies are *de facto* protection measures that distort market signals, while trade liberalization has the effect of readjusting prices, so enabling production to be localized in those regions with comparative advantages. Market access was their rallying cry, and they defended the most extreme liberalization positions. This crude free market position may have suited the developed country members of the Cairns Group, but by Cancún it had caused increasing tensions with the developing country members, who had most likely joined Cairns at the behest of the US, rather than based on the true interests of their own agricultural sectors. The Cairns Group virtually ceased to exist in Cancún, as its developing country members joined other coalitions. Indonesia and the Philippines joined the G33, while the big agro-exporters (Brazil, Chile, Thailand, Argentina, South Africa) went on to play key roles in the G20.

[handwritten margin note: firm free traders]

ACP

The ACP is a group of 79 African, Caribbean and Pacific states that receive preferential market access to the EU under the Lomé conventions. They fear that WTO negotiations will lead both to the rapid elimination of their tariff barriers, and to the gradual elimination of the EU preferential treatment they enjoy.

G10

A group of countries which support the concept of multifunctionality. According to this concept, agriculture is about more than producing commodities, it is also about preserving landscapes and protecting farm livelihoods and rural traditions, and it is about food security, and thus deserves special consideration in trade agreements. Multifunctionality was originally championed by the EU, which has since downplayed it as it brought too much conflict and led the US and the Cairns Group to accuse the EU of hypocritically defending its own farmers while subsidizing exports that undercut farmers elsewhere (one can convincingly argue that the criticizers were just as hypocritical, shedding crocodile tears for farmers who were also being hurt by cheap exports from the US and Cairns Group countries.) The G10 countries are net food-importing, mainly developed countries, including Bulgaria, Taiwan, South Korea, Iceland, Israel, Japan, Liechtenstein, Mauritius, Norway and Switzerland. They defend, among other things, the economic and cultural integrity of their rural regions, and value their countrysides and food quality highly. They are also concerned with price fluctuations. For Japan, Korea and Norway, whose food is largely imported, food security is regarded as a public good. To them it would be unacceptable to make their food supply totally dependent on the vagaries of the international market, or on political or economic pressures. The irrigated rice countries, like Japan and Korea, additionally stress the relationship between agriculture and the environment through the paddy landscape. According to the G10, these considerations justify an active role for government in the regulation of externalities and in the production of public goods. The G10 has expressed concern about the NG5 (see below) cutting deals behinds the backs of other nations, because it implies the political ownership of the negotiations by the large agro-export countries.

G20

This group was widely perceived by the media as having 'stood up to' the US and EU in Cancún (though the reality is that virtually all of the groups listed here stood up to the US and EU, causing the collapse of the talks), and in Hong Kong as well. The current members include major agro-exporters Brazil, Argentina, South Africa, Thailand, Chile, and China, and potentially major agro-exporters like India. India, Brazil and China have taken the lead, and defend net trade liberalization aimed at opening up market access in the US and EU for their exports. The G20 has also attracted a group of countries whose own interests are less clearly aligned solely with agro-exports (though many of them do have politically powerful agro-export elites), but who nevertheless were drawn to the perceived strong opposition to the North. These include Bolivia, Cuba, Egypt, India, Indonesia, Mexico, Nigeria, Pakistan, Paraguay, Philippines, Tanzania, Venezuela and Zimbabwe. The G20 proudly claims to represent half of the world's population and two-thirds of its farmers, though its positions clearly favor the tiny agro-export elite among those farmers. The G20's negotiating position is simple: increased access to the Northern markets for G20 agricultural products, an end to agricultural export subsidies, and the elimination of domestic supports that are effectively export subsidies. By putting a much higher priority on opening export markets than on protecting domestic markets, the G20 position is actually much closer to the US/EU position than to the positions advocated by family farmer and peasant organizations within the G20 countries: this is why the G20 has been repudiated by Via Campesina, the global alliance of family farm and peasant groups. Paul Nicholson, of the Via Campesina International Coordinating Committee, said: 'No one should think for a moment that if Argentina can export more tons of soy to the EU that even one less Argentine child will die of hunger, when it is precisely the expansion of soy and other crops for export by large landowners that is displacing family farmers into misery and hunger.'

G33

The G33 is also known as the Alliance on Special Products and a Special Safeguard Mechanism (SP/SSM Alliance). This Group is made up of 42 developing country members of the WTO, and includes Antigua and Barbuda, Barbados, Belize, Benin, Botswana, China, Congo, Cuba, Dominican Republic, Grenada, Guyana, Haiti, Honduras, India, Indonesia, Ivory Coast, Jamaica, Kenya, Korea, Mauritius, Mongolia, Montserrat, Mozambique, Nicaragua, Nigeria, Pakistan, Panama, The Philippines, Peru, Saint Kitts, Saint Lucia, Saint Vincent and the Grenadines, Senegal, Sri Lanka, Suriname, Tanzania, Trinidad and Tobago, Turkey, Uganda, Venezuela, Zambia and Zimbabwe. This group wants to have the right to self-designate sensitive 'special products,' for which they would not have to cut tariffs. Over the three years previous to Cancún, development concerns regarding agriculture (the impact of rapid import liberalization on small farmers) gave rise to a proposal for a 'development box' in the Agreement on Agriculture. Eventually this controversial discussion in turn produced a proposal to enable developing countries to protect vulnerable farmers by granting these countries additional tariff flexibility on a range of special products (SPs) of particular importance to food security and rural development, and to be provided with a special safeguard mechanism (SSM) to deal with import surges across all products.

G77

The G77 was established in 1964 by 77 developing countries at the end of the first session of the United Nations Conference on Trade and Development (UNCTAD) in Geneva, and is the largest Third World coalition in the United Nations. Although the membership of the G77 has increased to 132 countries, the original name was retained because of its historic significance. The G77 believe in the role of UNCTAD in regulating trade in commodities, and in strong multilateralism in general.

G90

The G90, formed at Cancún, is made up of the 79-state Africa, Caribbean and Pacific (ACP) bloc, the African Union, and the nations known collectively as the least-developed countries (LDCs). Of course, 'G90' is an exaggeration, since if one stops double-counting the members of two or three of the above groupings, it includes only 61 WTO members. The G90 expresses concerns over the need for enhanced access to developed country markets (similar to the G20); self-selection of so-called 'special products' for developing countries (similar to the G33), and the need to compensate for the erosion of trade preferences (breaks on tariffs) that the poorest countries often get in the US and EU, once (and if) the trade superpowers begin reducing their tariffs for everybody (thus the poorest would lose the advantage they currently enjoy). The G90 also strongly backed the demand of several African countries that the US slash its cotton subsidies. Some G90 members want no tariff cuts in their own countries, for at least the poorest among them, or at least for developing countries to be able to keep some level of tariffs, with a preferential margin for G90 members.

G120

The G120 bloc emerged in Hong Kong and is composed of the G20, G33, ACP, LDCs, the African Group and the Small Economies group. It includes 120 countries and covers four-fifths of the world's population. It is a sort of 'least-common denominator' group that tries to 'harmonize' minimum common positions. They want all export supports gone by 2010, they want to address some specific needs of LDCs and G33 countries, and they focus on issues of market access and on countries that receive preferences, on LDC demands for quota- and duty-free access to Northern markets, and on the West Africa cotton issue.

NG5/FIP

The so called 'Non-Group of Five Members,' *aka* the Five Interested Parties (FIP), has emerged in post-Cancún negotiations, and includes the US, EU, Australia, Brazil and India. These are the countries that serve as leaders of the different pro-trade liberalization negotiating blocs within the WTO: the United States and the European Union, Brazil and India – representing the G20 developing countries – and Australia, which coordinates the more or less defunct Cairns Group. The function of the NG5 appears to be to reach agreements, behind closed doors, that benefit agro-exporters, and which the five can then seek to impose on the rest of the world.

[handwritten annotation: "Is there any back up to back this up?"]

Where European and American Family Farmers Stand

WTO Agricultural Negotiations in Geneva

A joint statement by the European Farmers Coordination (CPE) and the National Family Farm Coalition, USA (NFFC).[132]

The current drive to reach agreement on agricultural issues at the World Trade Organization (WTO) should be brought to a halt. The WTO General Council is meeting in Geneva to discuss a framework on agriculture that is completely unacceptable. We propose a new EU agriculture policy, a new US Farm Bill, and new international trade rules, all based on food sovereignty and sustainable family farming.

The European Union and the United States must put an end to the swindle they have been imposing on other WTO members since the Uruguay Round of the GATT in 1994. Who can believe the sincerity of the European Union and the United States when their stated intentions to end export subsidies only results in letting internal prices drop to extremely low 'world levels,' thus dumping US and EU commodities on the export market to the detriment of farmers all over the world?

Propping up the US and EU agricultural systems with massive amounts of direct payments re-categorized as Green Box or Blue Box payments fails miserably in concealing the duplicity of the EU, US and the multinational agribusiness corporations that benefit from buying low-priced commodities. The claims by these corporations that cheap commodities benefit consumers is belied by their ever-increasing profit margins, the destruction of local food systems, and growing populations of undernourished citizens. Likewise claims of benefits to US and EU farmers are belied by the loss of family farms, the growth of industrialized livestock production and the de-population of the countryside in the United States and the EU.

Export subsidies, public support, taxpayer's money

Both the EU and the US are attempting to justify and maintain their current subsidy systems by simply re-categorizing payments, which carries the illusion that they are decreasing export subsidies with the expectation that a greater agricultural balance will arise between developing and developed countries. This is not the case. The apparent rationale of the EU and the US to diminish trade distorting domestic support unfortunately parallels the misguided efforts of the Cairns group and the G20 to discredit the importance of government involvement in achieving social and environmental justice in the world's many agricultural systems.

Public support in agriculture is legitimate, in the South as in the North, provided that it does not serve to promote production or exports at prices below production costs. But it is precisely one of the objectives of the EU/US direct payments – to allow all production (for domestic use and for export) to be priced at extremely low 'world prices.'

Market access

We believe that the benefits of 'market access' are illusory goals for the benefit of the family farmers of developing countries. As the common statement of Via Campesina and ROPPA (Africa) indicated in May 2001, 'In less developed countries, the first priority of farmers is to produce for their families, then to seek access to their domestic market, before seeking to export.' The international pricing of commodities, the advantage of destructive industrial techniques in developed countries, and the exclusivity of market arrangements with multinational trading corporations will eliminate most family farmers in developing countries from any benefits whatsoever. This is not a picture of broad-based development or democratic participation.

Who actually benefits from the export-oriented market access solution?

The first beneficiaries are a handful of business elites and the landed oligarchy in developing countries that have the technology and political connections to profit from market access. They are supported by structural adjustment programs of the World Bank that require developing countries to repay their burdensome debts to multinational banks. This export-oriented agriculture benefits the privileged few and leads to further underdevelopment rather than development with a view to the future.

The second group of beneficiaries includes multinational agribusiness corporations that benefit from expanded access to cheap inputs and new markets to be served by their reliance on industrial processing and retailing techniques. Local markets and customary activities are destroyed. These corporations have also started to move their agricultural production from the North to less developed countries (from US to Mexico, from EU to South America, Africa, etc.) to benefit from cheap labor and land.

Continuing down this path will lead to the loss of sustainable family farm based agriculture around the world, including in the EU and US. Cheap feed grains and protein meal already have led to the destruction of diversified family farms with replacement by inhumane and polluting livestock factories often owned or controlled by multinational corporations.

More and more farmers and governments in developing countries, together with the CPE and NFFC, are saying, 'No!' to further 'trade liberalization' under WTO which will be so destructive to their society, culture, and environment. We demand that our governments stop the intense political and economic pressure being exerted on them to comply with EU and US WTO policies that result in the curse of low commodity prices intensifying the rural crisis, urban congestion, and unemployment.

Thus, CPE and NFFC demand that the European Union and the United States abandon their current agricultural and trade policies. The rules of international agricultural trade must be based on the right to food sovereignty, which excludes any form of dumping but allows countries to develop their own domestic food and agricultural policy. Current WTO rules and the latest EU and US demands will result in cultural, environmental and social costs that cannot be measured by 'domestic support formulas.' While only 10 per cent of the world's agricultural production enters international trade, the imposition of the WTO on agricultural policies threatens to preclude a democratic peaceful world for current and future generations.

In May 2004, CPE and NFFC, along with Via Campesina, ROPPA, and other organizations launched an international campaign to change the EU Common Agricultural Policy (CAP) so that it is in line with people's food sovereignty. The US Farm Bill must also embrace food sovereignty, and, likewise, reflect the importance of sustainable family farming at home and abroad.

We, CPE and NFFC, declare that the EU needs a new Common Agricultural Policy and the US needs a new Farm Bill based on food sovereignty and sustainable family farming, as follows:

- Remunerative farm prices related to production costs rather than a reliance on income from government payments;

- Supply management on an international, national, and regional level. This will include the necessity of excluding cheap imports that threaten price support and supply management mechanisms;

- Suppression of any form of subsidies for export or those intended to encourage production for export; → *but will perpetuate overprod. bus. costs* ?

- A public support system, which ensures the maintenance of agricultural production in less favored areas, develops socially and environmentally sustainable, sound production methods, and local processing and retailing of products;

- Structural measures that halt and reverse the concentration of production in large factory farms, including industrial livestock factories that are devastating the countryside;

- Give priority to the entry of young farmers into agriculture.

Where Peasant and Family Farm Organizations Stand

It is Urgent to Re-Orient the Debate on Agriculture and Initiate a Policy of Food Sovereignty
A STATEMENT BY LA VIA CAMPESINA[133]

We call on all those responsible in governments to step out of the 'neoliberal model' and to have the courage to seek an alternative path of cooperation with social justice and mutual assistance.

The failure of the WTO [in Cancún] was the failure of actors who are totally locked in a 'neoliberal mindset'. Those responsible for trade orient themselves principally to the interests of the elite and transnational industries. They appear to be incapable of seeing the real problems, much less seeking solutions for them. They think only of increased trade, grabbing bigger market shares, more privatization, more accumulation and more profit. Their only concern in the agricultural sector is to deal with export interests. This is shameful given the fact that the existence of millions and millions of peasants, more than half the world's population, depends on local and domestic production and marketing.

La Vía Campesina believes that we need to engage in this debate. We must define more clearly the existing problems and articulate much-needed solutions. We must also include those who are more responsible in governments and international institutions and who, we hope, are more sensitive to the real challenges of our world. The true conflict is not between governments, it is between models of production.

Because of the scandalous behavior of certain Northern governments in defending the interests of transnational industries, the conflict in Cancún was portrayed as a 'North–South' conflict. We applaud the resistance of many governments, above all, of the South, against the dominance and the imposition of the United States (US), the European Union (EU) and some other industrialized countries. Nevertheless, we reiterate that in the agricultural sector, the real conflict behind this confrontation among governments is a conflict between a sustainable model of peasant production based on food sovereignty, demanded by the peasants in the North and South, and an industrial model, oriented to export, pushed for by transnationals, the US, the EU, other industrialized countries, but also by certain elite and important forces within governments of the South.

We hope to be able to begin a dialogue with governments of the South and the North. We propose to take concrete steps to limit the damaging effects of the industrial-exporting model and to strengthen sustainable peasant production.

The first important step: we must center the debate on food sovereignty and production rather than trade.

To engage in agricultural production that ensures food needs, respects the environment and provides peasants with a life of dignity, an active intervention by the government is indispensable. This intervention must ensure:

- peasants' and small-scale farmers' access to the means of production (land, seed, water, credit);

- control of imports in order to stabilize the internal price to a level that covers the costs of production;

- control of production (i.e. supply management) in order to avoid surpluses;

- international commodity agreements to control supply and guarantee fair prices to peasant producers for export products such as coffee, cotton, etc.;

- public assistance to help the development of peasant production and marketing;

- organization of the domestic market to give local peasant women and men full access to this market.

To take concrete steps in this direction we must urgently explore alternatives at the national and international levels. We call on the agencies of the UN such as the FAO, the UNCTAD and the ILO to take initiatives to develop an alternative framework to the WTO. This alternative framework must seek to redefine international agricultural policies that address the poverty and marginalization that characterize the majority living in rural areas.

Cheap imports have disastrous effects. To obtain food sovereignty it is essential to stop dumping.
Worldwide, agricultural imports at low prices are destroying local agricultural economies. Prior to Cancún and at the behest of the United States and the European Union, the WTO ratified a new dumping practice. In the European Union, internal prices above world market level combined with export subsidies are being replaced by low internal agricultural prices and direct (decoupled) payments. These payments continue to the largest producers. In the US similar mechanisms are put in place. These policies continue and exacerbate dumping. It gives an enormous advantage to agribusiness. It also discredits agricultural subsidies in general which, in turn, negatively affects the possibility of maintaining much needed public financial support to peasant agriculture.

The answer to the dumping of surpluses is not 'to liberalize further.'
Eliminating direct and indirect export subsidies is an important step but even more important is a policy to control supply. Supply management effectively eliminates surpluses. Effective supply

management also allows prices covering the cost of production and public financial support to peasant agriculture without generating surpluses that are dumped on other markets. The response to certain industrialized countries that practice dumping, cannot be to demand more liberalization and even more access to markets. These proposals do not defend the interest of farmers! Instead, these proposals only benefit export agriculture and transnationals (in the North and in the South); these proposals lead to the destruction of peasant production.

We must demand that surplus-producing countries limit their production and manage their supply in order to avoid excess production and subsequent dumping.

These countries should orient their public assistance to the development of sustainable peasant production geared for the internal market. Importing countries should have the right to stop imports to protect domestic production and invest in this sector.

'Free' trade with 'fair' competition is an illusion. Agricultural markets need strong state intervention.

The neoliberal logic claims that an unsubsidized agricultural market with no border regulation and with no state intervention will make optimal use of the comparative advantages, create more benefits for everyone and thus regulate itself in a fair way. However by their very nature, agricultural markets cannot function in a socially just way without intervention by the state. Ending state intervention by eliminating agriculture policy instruments one by one would perpetuate the destructive restructuring of agriculture. This will displace millions and millions of men and women peasants, leaving them with no way to make a living. Regions and entire countries would be left with no capacity to produce food. Finally, only those who have money to purchase food will be able to eat. This scenario is catastrophic and includes an immense loss in terms of local varieties and food products, peasant knowledge, agricultural biodiversity, etc.

Peasants, rural women and small farmers make up more than half the world's population. We have the right to a life of dignity. We have the right to produce our own food in our own territory. We have a right to make a living on our land.

A food sovereignty policy would make this possible. Sustainable peasant production can guarantee a better standard of living in rural areas, help limit damage to the environment, and it can create the necessary economic dynamics to contribute to development of countries.

Our Korean friend, Mr. Lee died in Cancún while defending food sovereignty. We hope that his death will not be in vain.

The WTO kills men and women peasants!
Let us take the path of food sovereignty!
WTO out of agriculture!

International Coordinating Committee, Via Campesina
Tegucigalpa, 11 November 2003

Food from Family Farms Act

A Proposal for the 2007 US
Farm Bill by the National Family Farm Coalition, USA[134]

*Crafted by family farmers to ensure fair prices for family farmers,
safe and healthy food, and vibrant, environmentally sound rural
communities here and around the world*

Why we need the Food from Family Farms Act

The goal of food, farm, and trade policy should be a globally sustainable and adequate supply of wholesome food at affordable prices. A family farm system is the most effective means to provide food quality and safety, diversity of production, equitable social and economic opportunity, and preservation of land, water, and biodiversity.

⊗ *but not affordability?*

However, family farmers everywhere are struggling economically. Farmers in this country and around the world are all urged to produce for the export market, only to find out that world market prices (as determined at commodity futures exchanges in cities like Chicago or New York) don't even cover production costs, much less family expenses. In addition, the low commodity prices don't reflect external costs, including damage to the environment, loss of rural economic opportunity, and community destruction. The global food system, while abundant, fails to feed the hungry, fails to promote healthful diets, and fails to eliminate food safety risks like disease pathogens and chemical contamination.

⊗ *what preserver exist?*

So-called free trade agreements like the North American Free Trade Agreement (NAFTA) and the World Trade Organization

(WTO) hamstring domestic US farm policy, thus destroying our sovereignty, in this case, food sovereignty. Fair prices to farmers cannot be guaranteed due to lack of mechanisms such as a price floor (or price support), food security reserves, and conservation set-asides. Billions of taxpayer dollars in annual subsidies cushion some of the losses for farmers in the US and in those few other countries who can afford to pay them, but wreak havoc in developing countries' rural sectors. Worldwide migration out of rural communities to overcrowded cities and across national borders creates unbelievable hardship.

The current system benefits multinational corporations: giant exporters, processors, and retailers, who profit by buying the cheapest commodities from all over the world, processing them and marketing them in monopolistic markets devoid of honest competition. Under-priced feed grains and oilseeds provide the main components of manufactured livestock feed. Corporate livestock and dairy production gain competitive advantage using cheap grain to the detriment of diversified family farmers who maintain crop rotations and recycle animal waste as crop nutrients. Labor-intensive fruit and vegetable production shifts to countries where workers have few rights and are paid $4 per day, causing unemployment and low wages for US farm workers.

Family farmers, farmworkers, and food-processing workers produce a necessity of life: they deserve dignity, justice, and equity rather than exploitation for corporate profit. Restoring farm income from the sale of farm commodities at a fair price must be the primary focus of any new farm program. Trade agreements should likewise respect a country's Food Sovereignty, the right to establish policies based on a country's needs and traditions for food security, conservation of natural resources and the geographical distribution of economic opportunity.

The National Family Farm Coalition has developed a new farm policy proposal to create a sustainable farm and food system. Our farm bill, called the Food from Family Farms Act (FFFA), would improve the environment, create new economic opportunities in rural America, and support similar aspirations in every other country on our beautiful planet. Unlike the current farm policy, provisions in the Food from Family Farms Act, predicated on the principle of Food Sovereignty, will build good will among our trading partners and give them a chance for balanced sustainable economic development.

The Food from Family Farms Act contains a price support system, food security reserves, and conservation set-asides with full planting flexibility, which would work together to guarantee prices that reflect the true cost of production. The Food from Family Farms Act encourages such a transition through full implementation of the Conservation Security Program (CSP), offering incentives on working lands for more conserving crops and practices which fit well with diversified family farming, bio-energy and local food production. A balanced family farm system will require less fossil fuel and give opportunities for farmers to become producers of clean renewable energy. In conjunction with the Food from Family Farms Act, the National Family Farm Coalition urges the US government to enforce anti-trust laws against increasing corporate concentration and vertical integration in the food industry from production and processing to marketing and retailing. The ownership of livestock by packing companies and their control of captive supplies must be banned because this gives them the power to encourage overproduction and manipulate markets to the detriment of family farmers and ranchers. Likewise, because these same multinational companies threaten to move livestock production overseas to avoid health and environmental regulation, consumers need mandatory country of origin labeling (COOL) of their food in all cases.

The USDA must respond to historical and ongoing civil rights complaints and implement laws that enable equitable access to farm and housing programs for all farmers and rural people. Farmers who produce under contract should have the right to fair arbitration clauses, contract transparency, and other rights currently denied. The USDA can promote new regional and local markets for farm products and purchases of food by federal agencies from independent family farms. The plight of America's migrant agricultural workers should be adequately addressed through its farm, labor, and trade policies.

vague

The Administration should change course in international trade towards cooperation in creating international commodity floor prices that are fair to all farmers, international food security reserves, and set-aside programs that encourage conservation and bioenergy production. Congress should respond to the popular demand for economic, environmental and social sustainability of the food system by enacting the Food from Family Farms Act.

Outline of bill

Food sovereignty

Trade and farm policy should respect every country's right to establish policies based on needs and traditions for food security, conservation of natural resources, and distribution of economic opportunity.

Prosperity for US farmers must not come at the expense of farmers and peasants in other nations. The United States must take the lead in promoting international commodity agreements aimed at setting floor prices and equitable sharing of responsibility for international reserves and supply management, thus eliminating the destructive practice of dumping.

The ability to develop farm programs that respond to the needs of our nation's farmers and consumers must be reinstated through adoption of provisions such as Section 22 of the Agricultural Adjustment Act. Section 22 allows for a limitation on imports of a specific commodity if that level disrupts the fair domestic market price for our nation's farmers.

Market price support

Farmers who comply with provisions of the Food from Family Farms Act (FFFA) will be eligible for market price supports established through a Commodity Credit Corporation (CCC) non-recourse loan for wheat, feed-grains, soybeans, oilseeds, cotton and rice. Loan rates will be set at an appropriate level that reflects the cost of production for each individual crop based on USDA's Economic Research Service (ERS) calculations and average transportation and storage costs. A similar formula will apply for establishing the price for milk at the farm-gate. The non-recourse loan creates an actual price floor requiring purchasers to pay at least the loan rate for commodities. If the purchaser won't pay the loan rate, the crop can be forfeited to a government reserve. This replaces the marketing loan of the 1996 Freedom to Farm bill and the 2002 Farm Bill that allow prices to drop below loan rates due to Loan Deficiency Payments (LDP) and Marketing Loan Gains.

Loans can be paid back with interest at any time when market conditions warrant. At the end of the nine-month loan period, producers will have the option of redeeming the loan, forfeiture to the CCC Food Security Reserve, or entry into the Farmer Owned Reserve (FOR), if open. A maximum quantity of crops up to a loan value of $450,000 per farm will be eligible for the loan program.

LDPs or marketing loan gains are no longer necessary. Storage costs on the FOR will be paid at the commercial rate with an annual payment in advance. Farmers will be allowed to rotate the commodities in the FOR to maintain quality. A low-interest loan program for construction of on-farm storage facilities will be established.

Reserves: food security, humanitarian, energy, and farmer-owned

Without a price support and reserves, a bountiful crop becomes an economic curse to farmers as overproduction can result in only one outcome: lower prices and economic hardship. The FFFA creates various reserves to enhance food, energy, and national security.

A Strategic Reserve stocked to a level of 7.5 per cent of the average annual use will have first priority with commodities forfeited from non-recourse loans. Half of the reserve can be used for emergency humanitarian relief and half can be used to supply the growing renewable fuels industry. (Under unusual circumstances, the Secretary may be allowed to buy stocks from the market for the Strategic Reserve.) Further forfeitures will fill a Food Security Reserve (FSR) set at a minimum 10 per cent of annual usage. No stocks from the FSR may enter the market until the Secretary determines that the national average price exceeds 150 per cent of the loan rate for 30 consecutive days. When the supplies in the FSR reach the 10 per cent of annual use, the Secretary will announce the opening of a FOR that allows farmers to extend the original non-recourse loan past 9 months, stop accrual of interest, and receive storage payments from CCC at commercial rates. Any stocks in the FSR above the minimum 10 per cent can be used by the Secretary to immediately replenish the strategic reserve. If free stocks become tight and drive national average market prices above 130 per cent of the loan rate for 30 consecutive days, storage payments cease on extended loans in the FOR. If national average market prices exceed 140% of the loan rate for 30 consecutive days, then the extended loans will be called for repayment.

Inventory management and conservation compliance

For farmers to be eligible for the price support loan program, along with other benefits of the FFFA, including cost share and disaster relief, they will be required to abide by the current Conservation Compliance. Because the nation's food security is assured by the existence of the FSR and FOR, the Secretary shall establish a short-term conservation set-aside program for program crops to avoid wasteful over production and balance production with demand. The Secretary shall target specific crops for reduced planting with the goal that production will satisfy projected demand. This includes supplies that will be needed to refill Strategic and Food Security reserves. Participating farmers will be required to idle a percentage of a target crop grown (Conservation Percentage (CP)) and enter into a soil-conservation program approved by the local Soil Conservation Service on those idled acres. After meeting that requirement, the producer/operator shall have flexibility to determine the crop mix to plant within the acreage base under this section.

Full planting flexibility within acreage base

Beyond idling the CP for each program crop, the farmer retains full planting flexibility on the Whole Farm Acreage Base which will be defined as Tillable Crop Acres – land that was planted or considered planted to programs crops in at least three of the five preceding crops.

Disaster program

The nation must recognize the importance of preserving the family farm system and therefore must provide an effective response when natural disasters strike family farms. Increased farm income from price supports at cost of production will be the first line of defense against economic catastrophe. The FFFA Disaster Program eliminates the current subsidized crop insurance system that is not only inadequate when disaster strikes but fosters production on marginal land and underwrites farm consolidation. In its place, a disaster relief program will be offered to all eligible farmers.

When a natural disaster generates a loss so that production is above 75 per cent of established yield, no payment will be made. When production is between 50 per cent and 75 per cent of established yield, payments (or grain from the Strategic Reserve above its 10 per cent minimum level) will be provided to replace income up to the 75 per cent level at 60 per cent loan rate value, not to exceed $67,500. Further production loss down to 30 per cent yield will be reimbursed at 75 per cent loan rate value, not to exceed

$67,500. Production loss below 30 per cent yield will be replaced at 100 per cent loan rate value, not to exceed $90,000. A loss of 90 per cent shall be considered a total loss and the producers shall have the right to salvage any remaining crop for whatever purpose they choose with no loss of disaster benefits. Insurance coverage from the private sector beyond established disaster relief would be at the producers' cost, but will not be required in order to qualify for the Disaster Program. Receiving crop insurance benefits will not disqualify a producer from receiving full disaster benefits under the disaster program.

Conservation security program

Sustainability must be the bedrock principle of agricultural reform, recognizing the benefits of diversified production versus the concentrated, intensive production in today's industrialized agricultural system. When livestock factories have to pay the full cost of production for their manufactured livestock feed, livestock production on family farms with more ecological crop rotations and use of animal manure for crop nutrients will become more economically viable. To reach our goal of sustainability and family farm diversity, the FFFA encourages such a transition through full implementation of the Conservation Security Program (CSP), offering incentives on working lands for more conserving crops and practices which fit well with diversified family farming and local food production.

Targeting

The FFFA is intended to reverse the current consolidation and industrialization of the nation's farms. Establishing fair prices through price supports and inventory management, thus internalizing costs experienced by farm families, the environment and rural society, is an essential step. Further, some benefits of the Food from Family Farms Act will be capped or targeted. The amount of commodities eligible for non-recourse loans will be based on a loan cap of $450,000 for all production under loan per crop year. Limits on payments in the disaster relief program will prevent the subsidized underwriting of farm expansion. Likewise, benefits of conservation programs like Environmental Quality Incentives Program (EQIP) and the CSP will target family farms rather than large industrial operations.

Increased funding of direct farm ownership and operating loans

Ownership of farms by family farmers helps ensure that they can meet their responsibility to conserve productive capacity and biodiversity for future generations. Federal and state programs to encourage entry into farming through access to affordable credit by beginning and minority farmers is critical. Historic discrimination against minority farmers by USDA must be reversed.

For a Legitimate, Sustainable and Supportive CAP

A Statement by the
European Farmers' Coordination (CPE)[135]

Why the CAP should be changed

The collapse of the Cancún WTO negotiations in September of 2003 clearly brought to light the deadlock of the European Union in its way of reforming the Common Agricultural Policy (CAP). The CAP needs to recover its international credibility and legitimacy.

By forcing the CAP reform decision a little bit on 26 June 2003, before Cancún, the European Commission clearly underestimated the refusal of third countries to tolerate any more what is a Euro-American 'swindle' invented at the beginning of the 1990s: decreasing the internal agricultural price to reach the world price, and combining it with direct payments (decoupling), with the supposed intention of boosting exports to the world market, while 'laundering' this new system thanks to the creation of the 'Green Box.'

The staple farm products from the EU and US go on being exported at an excessively low price, artificially curbed by direct payments. and often under the cost of production. What the EU calls 'reinforcing the competitiveness on the world market,' is nothing but an artifice linked to shifting the direct aid for exports – which disappears with the decrease of the European price – and replacing it with direct payments intended for a Green Box, which are only possible for rich countries.

The European Union has a great responsibility for the development of an international debate which tends to put all kinds of public support to agriculture into one and the same basket (that has to be eliminated). Public support to agriculture may well be legitimate, for instance so that sustainable family farming can exist in all the regions, provided that this support is not used for low-price exporting. Yet this is exactly the very core of the CAP reform implemented today. It is not possible to have a solid economy if it is based on providing products below the production costs.

In fact, the present rules of international trade and the CAP benefit the agri-food businesses, since they can get low-price supplies in Europe and also increasingly in the East or the South where they have relocated their subsidiaries (like the French company Doux in the poultry sector). These powerful economic stakeholders are the ones who need to have 'access to the' EU 'market.' The relocation of farm production outside Europe, by European companies, is on the move.

One example is the animal feedstuffs that have been imported since 1962 without customs duty. The massive imports of animal feedstuffs are the main reason for the existence of European meat and cereal surpluses, despite the fact that the EU does not have any real export vocation for these products.

The European Commission presents the 2003 CAP reform as a favorable reform for environment and animal welfare. Yet the intensive and industrialized production of poultry, pigs, beef and milk, based on massive imports of animal feedstuffs, has not been curbed, and in the last ten years decoupling of actual cereal production and direct payments has not reduced the amount of pesticides in underground waters. Producing at the lowest possible price cannot guarantee the multifunctional nature of agriculture, demanded by the European population. If we want that, then over-intensive production methods have to be changed, since they have many negative impacts.

The CAP must be legitimate in the eyes of European taxpayers. Therefore it is not possible to maintain a very unequal distribution of public funds in favor of big farms, of some sectors, in some regions. Yet the 2003 reform maintains these inequalities.

The CAP must therefore be reviewed. The issue is not to return to the old CAP, where after 1962, providing support to farm prices without any volume thresholds, granting export supports, giving up the community preference for animal feedstuffs, and the absence of supply management all led to the production of mountains of surpluses, over-intensive farming, concentration of production, and dumping *vis-à-vis* third countries.

Today the EU must escape from these contradictions and stop doing the opposite of what it says. Let us dare to develop sustainable family farming, as the population demands, which is multifunctional and non-distorting of the world market. It is a matter of the very survival of European agriculture.

Proposals

Our proposals are based on several key ideas and principles:

- The European Union would benefit a lot by maintaining sustainable family farming, not only for guaranteeing our food supply (food security), but also in terms of the social and multi-functional role of agriculture. The present trend must be reversed. Instead of concentrating farms in ever fewer hands, a fabric of small and medium-sized farms should be maintained. These farms play an irreplaceable role in: providing a quality and diversified food supply, landscape upkeep, wood and forest clearing, rural life, etc. Keeping people working in agriculture is not a sign of economic 'backwardness,' but is an added value for all.

- Each state or union of states has the right to define their own farm and food policies, as long as they do not disturb the international market: this is what is called food sovereignty.

- Any form of direct and indirect support for exports below their production costs (dumping) should be prohibited.

- The priority of the CAP should be to meet the needs of the internal market, and it should not be allowed any more to meet export interests first.

- In order to maintain the viability of agriculture in the long run, farmer income should be based on selling their own products. In other words, fair agricultural price should once again become the core element of income.

- For public support of farming to have strong social legitimacy, it must be distributed in a fair way among different farms, sectors, and countries, and production methods should be sustainable.

1. MAINTAINING FAMILY FARMING WITHOUT DISTURBING THE INTERNATIONAL MARKET: AGRICULTURAL PRICES, INCOME, AND TRADE

The EU does not have a real export vocation or natural excess productive capacity for staple animal products, milk and cereals. Therefore the export-driven trend, through the depression of internal farm prices, can just as well be given up. Then it will be possible to prioritize production for the internal market, remove all export subsidies, and manage the supply on the internal market.

If consumers want to maintain agricultural production in Europe, then farmers should be kept on this continent. For that purpose, since production costs are higher in the European region than in many other regions of the world, the market should be protected from low price imports, and this will become legitimate on the international level as soon as the EU stops its own low price exports. The EU should establish a Community preference level for all farm produce, including animal feedstuffs, which will be used as an orientation price for the European market. This level should be linked to an average European production cost[136] that meets sustainable conditions of production, and it must be reviewed on a regular basis.

If European citizens and taxpayers want to keep farmers in all the regions, including the less favored areas, they must allow them to produce, while supporting them through direct payment of the difference between their higher production cost and the level chosen for the Community preference. There would then be price-complementary direct payments, regrouped in one single payment per farm, with a ceiling determined according to the number of people working on the farm, taking into account the different products of the farm.

To sum up, the income linked to farm production would first be made up of the sales of farm products, given a European market price linked to European production costs, to which a direct payment can be added, variable according to regions.

For the European market to be able to maintain such a fair farm price, it is of course necessary to have supply management.

2. SUPPLY MANAGEMENT, SUSTAINABLE PRODUCTION METHODS

The objectives of sustainability and supply management are intertwined. Taking into consideration the external costs for society of over-intensive agricultural production methods, we need to de-intensify these over-intensive farms. What is needed is a transition period where financial support is provided to small and medium-sized farms. allowing the implementation of the following measures and instruments (this is a non-exhaustive list):

- maximum animal production should be linked to the area in fodder on the farm, via a progressive renunciation of industrial animal production,

- strict application of the nitrates directive (which must be improved),

- prohibition of antibiotics in feedstuffs,

- prohibition of straw shorteners,

- encourage farms to use fewer external inputs, to practice the crop rotation, to replace maize for silage in Northern Europe by mixing grass with leguminous plants,

- support irrigation only in dry zones, when groundwater is in not endangered, and for crops which absolutely need irrigation,

- stop public support for drainage,

- support those farms which respect stricter environmental standards and preserve biodiversity,

- implement animal production standards which respect animal welfare,

- temporary specific support for production of vegetable protein on livestock farms,

- training and research directed toward sustainable family farming.

These measures, dealing with de-intensification, as well as a Community preference applied on animal feedstuffs, will eliminate the present structural surpluses of animal products and cereal. However, in case of circumstantial surpluses (sustainable farming remains dependent upon climatic factors), other complementary measures are necessary, such as establishing a minimum farm purchasing price for agribusiness.

3. TO FAVOUR REGIONAL MARKETS AND THE LOCAL PROCESSING OF PRODUCTS

EAGGF and structural funds should support local and regional markets, direct marketing at the farm (instead of promoting products for export), and small-scale local food processing, instead of supporting the concentration of slaughter-houses or the building of giant export infrastructure like harbours and highways.

4. QUALITY AND SAFETY OF AGRICULTURAL PRODUCTS

- A general ban of GMOs in food production, food processing, and imports.

- Authorized products in animal feedstuffs should be registered in a positive list, with full labelling regarding composition and origin.

- The emission and the presence of toxic products in food, such as dioxins, nitrofuranes, heavy metals and antibiotics, should be monitored in a stricter way and both of these phenomena should be prohibited over the long term.

- Upstream and downstream food-processing companies have to be made legally and financially responsible for the consequences of their industrial practices on human and animal health, and the environment.

- Quality standards should be revised, giving priority to the interests of consumers and not of agribusiness.

5. FOR RURAL LIFE

Without an active European policy which supports young and new farmers from settling in rural areas, the countryside will continue to lose its farmers. We need urgently:

- to ban the sale of production rights and quotas,

- to stop the repurchase of the farm by each generation (in some countries),

- to fix maximum investment ceilings, rather than set minimum areas for receiving support: we prefer *'neighbours to hectares.'*

In order to limit the concentration of land in the hands of ever fewer and larger farms, the member states must implement measures allowing the priority allocation of land to small farms and people who want to settle as farmers.

To reverse the current regional overconcentration of agricultural production, we must push a relocalization of production of products in regions where it is their natural or cultural vocation (but where they have disappeared or regressed). Pig and sheep production in less-favoured areas is a good example.

6. INTERNATIONAL MARKETS WITHOUT DUMPING

'Food sovereignty is the RIGHT of countries/unions of countries to decide their own agriculture and food policy, without dumping regarding third countries.' – Via Campesina

The different regions of the world have regional products to trade, and the world needs fair rules for these exchanges. But this must be done without economic dumping (exporting below production costs) or social and environmental dumping. Priority should not be given any more to exporting low-price staple products, but to local and regional food production. It is a matter of narrowing down the international agricultural and trade negotiations to commerce and not letting them define the agricultural polices, as it is the case today.

The policy described above will put the European Union in a better position for negotiating and making alliances, since the EU would have abandoned direct and indirect export support. The EU would be better able to justify the Community preference and the right of all the countries/groups of countries to protect themselves from excessively low-price imports.

The WTO should not be able to dictate farm or public service policies (health, education, water, energy, etc.). Trade rules should be subordinated to the Universal Declaration of Human Rights and the international conventions on social and environmental issues. UNCTAD, in connection with the FAO, should be reinstated in its functions in order to deal with agricultural trade rules, and an international independent legal body should be set up in order to settle trade disputes.

Immediate measures

1 A fairer allocation method for direct payments to farmers. The historical basis chosen for setting up the direct payments is not legitimate for the taxpayers, who in this way go on financing mainly the big agricultural and animal farms. It is necessary to rebalance public support among all these farms, production sectors and countries, focusing the support mainly on the small and medium-sized farms, which guarantee a living countryside. A ceiling for direct payments per farm is indispensable, taking into account the number of people who work on the farm.

2 Banning the sale of rights to produce and rights to direct payments, which favors speculation and make things even more difficult for people who want to settle as farmers.

3 Adopting the zero GMO contamination rates for seeds, otherwise GMO dissemination will be unavoidable.

4 Maintaining the GMO moratorium.

5 Not increasing the European dairy quota, since the EU already has a surplus in this sector.

6 In case of circumstantial crisis, adopting minimum farm produce purchase prices for agribusiness and mass marketing.

People's Food Sovereignty Statement[137]

La Via Campesina and the People's Food Sovereignty Network

Food and agriculture are fundamental to all peoples, in terms of both production and availability of sufficient quantities of safe and healthy food, and as foundations of healthy communities, cultures and environments. All of these are being undermined by the increasing emphasis on neoliberal economic policies promoted by leading political and economic powers, such as the United States (US) and the European Union (EU), and realized through global institutions, such as the World Trade Organization (WTO), International Monetary Fund (IMF) and the World Bank (WB). Instead of securing food for the peoples of the world, these institutions have presided over a system that has prioritized export-oriented production, increased global hunger and malnutrition, and alienated millions from productive assets and resources such as land, water, fish, seeds, technology and know-how. Fundamental change to this global regime is urgently required.

People's food sovereignty is a right

In order to guarantee the independence and food sovereignty of all of the world's peoples, it is essential that food is produced though diversified, community-based production systems. Food sovereignty is the right of peoples to define their own food and agriculture; to protect and regulate domestic agricultural production and trade in order to achieve sustainable development objectives; to determine the extent to which they want to be self-reliant; to restrict the dumping of products in their markets; and to provide local fisheries-based communities the priority in managing the use of and the rights to aquatic resources. Food sovereignty does not negate trade, but rather, it promotes the formulation of trade policies and practices that serve the rights of peoples to safe, healthy and ecologically sustainable production.

Governments must uphold the rights of all peoples to food sovereignty and security, and adopt and implement policies that promote sustainable, family-based production rather than industry-led, high-input and export-oriented production. This in turn demands that they put in place the following measures:

Market policies

- Ensure adequate remunerative prices for all farmers and fishers;

- Exercise the rights to protect domestic markets from imports at low prices;

- Regulate production on the internal market in order to avoid the creation of surpluses;

- Abolish all direct and indirect export supports; and

- Phase out domestic production subsidies that promote unsustainable agriculture, inequitable land tenure patterns and destructive fishing practices; and support integrated agrarian reform programmes, including sustainable farming and fishing practices.

Food safety, quality and the environment

- Adequately control the spread of diseases and pests while at the same time ensuring food safety;

- Protect fish resources from both land-based and sea-based threats, such as pollution from dumping, coastal and off-shore mining, degradation of river mouths and estuaries and harmful industrial aquaculture practices that use antibiotics and hormones;

- Ban the use of dangerous technologies, such as food irradiation, which lower the nutritional value of food and create toxins in food;

- Establish food quality criteria appropriate to the preferences and needs of the people;

- Establish national mechanisms for quality control of all food products so that they comply with high environmental, social and health quality standards; and

- Ensure that all food inspection functions are performed by appropriate and independent government bodies, and not by private corporations or contractors.

Access to productive resources

- Recognize and enforce communities' legal and customary rights to make decisions concerning their local, traditional resources, even where no legal rights have previously been allocated;

- Ensure equitable access to land, seeds, water, credit and other productive resources;

- Grant the communities that depend on aquatic resources common property rights, and reject systems that attempt to privatize these public resources;

- Prohibit all forms of patenting of life or any of its components, and the appropriation of knowledge associated with food and agriculture through intellectual property rights regimes; and

- Protect farmers', indigenous peoples' and local community rights over plant genetic resources and associated knowledge – including farmers' rights to exchange and reproduce seeds.

Production–consumption

Develop local food economies based on local production and processing, and the development of local food outlets.

Genetically modified organisms (GMOs)

- Ban the production of, and trade in genetically modified (GM) seeds, foods, animal feeds and related products;

- Ban genetically modified foods to be used as food aid;

- Expose and actively oppose the various methods (direct and indirect) by which agribusiness corporations such as Monsanto, Syngenta, Aventis/Bayer and DuPont are bringing GM crop varieties into agricultural systems and environments; and

- Encourage and promote alternative agriculture and organic farming, based on indigenous knowledge and sustainable agriculture practices.

Transparency of information and corporate accountability

- Provide clear and accurate labelling of food and feed-stuff products based on consumers' and farmers' rights to access to information about content and origins;

- Establish binding regulations on all companies to ensure transparency, accountability and respect for human rights and environmental standards;

- Establish anti-trust laws to prevent the development of industrial monopolies in the food, fisheries and agricultural sectors; and

- Hold corporate entities and their directors legally liable for corporate breaches of environmental and social laws, and of national and international laws and agreements.

Specific protection of coastal communities dependent on marine and inland fish

- Prevent the expansion of shrimp aquaculture and the destruction of mangroves;

- Ensure local fishing communities have the rights to the aquatic resources;

- Negotiate a legally binding international convention to prevent illegal, unregulated and unreported fishing;

- Effectively implement international marine agreements and conventions, such as the UN Fish Stocks Agreement; and

- Eradicate poverty and ensure food security for coastal communities through equitable and sustainable community-based natural resource use and management, founded on indigenous and local knowledge, culture and experience.

an ambitious policy

Trade rules must guarantee food sovereignty

Global trade must not be afforded primacy over local and national developmental, social, environmental and cultural goals. Priority should be given to affordable, safe, healthy and good quality food, and to culturally appropriate subsistence production for domestic, sub-regional and regional markets. Current modes of trade liberalization, which allows market forces and powerful trans-national corporations (TNCs) to determine what and how food is produced, and how food is traded and marketed, cannot fulfil these crucial goals.

'No' to neoliberal policies in food and agriculture

The undersigned denounce the 'liberalization' of farm product exchanges as promoted through bilateral and regional free trade agreements, and multilateral institutions such as the IMF, the World Bank and the WTO. We condemn the dumping of food products in all markets, and especially in Third World countries where it has severely undermined domestic production. We condemn the attempts by the WTO and other multilateral institutions to sell all rights of aquatic resources to transnational consortiums. Neoliberal policies coerce countries into specializing in agricultural production in which they have a so-called 'comparative advantage' and then trading along the same lines. However, export-orientated production is being pushed at the expense of domestic food production, and production means and resources are increasingly controlled by large transnational corporations. The same is occurring in the fishing sector. Fishing communities are losing their rights of access to fisheries, because access has been transferred to industrial corporations, such as PESCANOVA. Those TNCs have consolidated a great part of the production and of the global fishing commerce.

Rich governments continue to heavily subsidize export-oriented agricultural and fisheries production in their countries, with the bulk of support going to large producers. The majority of taxpayers' funds are handed out to big business – large producers, traders and retailers – who engage in unsustainable agricultural, fisheries and trading practices, and not to small-scale family producers who produce much of the food for the internal market, often in more sustainable ways.

These export-oriented policies have resulted in market prices for commodities that are far lower than their real costs of production. This has encouraged and perpetuated dumping, and provided TNCs with opportunities to buy cheap products, which are then sold at significantly higher prices to consumers in both the North and the South. The larger parts of important agricultural and fisheries subsidies in rich countries are in fact subsidies for corporate agri-industry, traders, retailers and a minority of the largest producers.

The adverse effects of these policies and practices are becoming clearer every day. They lead to the disappearance of small-scale family farms and fishing communities in both the North and South; poverty has increased, especially in the rural areas; soils and water have been polluted and degraded; biological diversity has been lost, and natural habitats destroyed.

Dumping

Dumping occurs when goods are sold at less than their cost of production. This can be the result of subsidies and structural distortions, such as monopoly control over markets and distribution. The inability of current economic policy to factor in externalities, such as the depletion of water and soil nutrients and pollution resulting from industrial agricultural methods, also contributes to dumping. Dumping under the current neoliberal policies is conducted in North–South, South–North, South–South and North–North trade. Whatever the form, dumping ruins small-scale local producers in both the countries of origin and sale. For example:

- Imports by India of dairy surpluses subsidized by the European Union had negative impacts on local, family-based dairy production.

- Exports of industrial pork from the USA to the Caribbean proved ruinous to Caribbean producers;

- Imports by Ivory Coast of European pork at subsidized prices are three times lower than the production costs in Ivory Coast;

- Chinese exports of silk threads to India at prices far lower than the costs of production in India has been seriously damaging for hundreds of thousands of farmer families in Southern India; and

- On one hand the import of cheap maize from the US to Mexico – the centre of the origin of maize – ruins Mexican producers; on the other hand the export of vegetables at low prices from Mexico to Canada ruins producers in Canada. Dumping practices must be stopped. Countries must be able to protect their home markets against dumping and other trade practices that prove damaging to local producers. Exporting countries must not be allowed to dump surpluses on the international market, and should respond to real demands for agricultural goods and products in ways that do not undermine domestic production, but rather support and strengthen local economies.

There is no 'world market' of agricultural products

The so-called 'world market' of agricultural products does not exist. What exists is, above all, an international trade of surpluses of milk, cereals and meat dumped primarily by the EU, the US and other members of the Cairns group. Behind the faces of national trade negotiators are powerful TNCs, such as Monsanto and Cargill. They are the real beneficiaries of domestic subsidies and supports, international trade negotiations and the global manipulations of trade regimes. At present, international trade in agricultural products involves only 10 per cent of total worldwide agricultural production and is mainly an exchange between TNCs from the US, EU and a few other industrialized countries. The so called 'world market price' is extremely unstable and has no relation to the costs of production. It is far too low because of dumping, and therefore, it is not an appropriate or desirable reference for agricultural production.

The older siblings of the WTO: the World Bank and the IMF

The World Bank and the International Monetary Fund (IMF) are the older siblings of the WTO and serve as domestic arms of the WTO regime in developing countries. They have played significant roles in weakening agricultural autonomy, dismantling domestic self-sufficiency, creating famines and undermining food sovereignty. Their structural adjustment programmes – now called poverty reduction programmes – have created and entrenched policy-induced poverty across the developing world. Hardest hit by these policies are those who rely on agriculture and the natural environment for their livelihood and survival.

Despite mounting evidence to the contrary, the Bank and Fund are unchanged in their belief that 'global integration' of domestic agriculture systems and 'market access' are the best avenues to reduce poverty. Developing countries are exhorted to undertake reforms in their respective agriculture sectors, which include dismantling of agriculture subsidies, deregulation of pricing and distribution, privatization of agriculture support and extension services, provision of greater market access to foreign producers and removing all barriers to international agriculture trade. However, the Bank and Fund are unable to force the rich countries of the OECD to do the same. As a result, Bank-Fund policies entrench inequalities among the developed and developing world and reproduce colonial structures of production and distribution.

Privatization, liberalization and deregulation are the hallmarks of the World Bank-IMF approach to development and are necessary conditions in all Bank-Fund lending programmes. Despite fierce criticism from numerous farmers' organizations, academics and independent researchers, the Bank continues to support 'market-assisted land reform' and the creation of 'functioning land markets' as a key rural development strategy. Bank-Fund policies mandate the transformation of subsistence-based, community-oriented and self-sufficient agriculture systems to commercial and market-dependent production and distribution systems. Food crops are replaced by cash crops for export, and communities and societies are compelled to rely on external markets that they have no control over for food security. Furthermore, the emphasis on export crops has led to increased dependence on harmful and costly chemical inputs that threaten soil, water and air quality, biodiversity, and human and animal health, while providing greater profits for large agribusiness and chemical corporations.

The commercialization of agriculture has resulted in the consolidation of agricultural land and assets in the hands of agribusiness and other large commercial entities, displacing small-scale and family farmers off their lands to seek employment in off-farm activities, or as seasonal labour in the commercial agriculture sector. Most farmers in developing countries are steeped in debt as a result of increasing input costs and falling farm-gate prices for their products. Many have mortgaged their land and assets to repay old debts, and in several cases have lost their lands altogether. An equally large number have moved to contract farming for large agribusiness in order to hold on to whatever assets they have left. This has resulted in widespread migration of farming families, the creation of new pockets of poverty and inequality in rural and urban areas, and the fragmentation of entire rural communities.

The World Bank and the IMF threaten the wealth, diversity and potential of our agriculture. Agriculture is not simply an economic sector, it is a complex of ecosystems and processes that include forests, rivers, plains, coastal areas, biodiversity, human and animal habitats, production, distribution, consumption, conservation, etc. Bank-Fund policies are creeping into every one of these areas. In order to protect our agriculture, the World Bank and the IMF must be removed from food and agriculture altogether.

The World Trade Organization dismisses calls for reform

The WTO is undemocratic and unaccountable, has increased global inequality and insecurity, promotes unsustainable production and consumption patterns, erodes diversity and undermines social and environmental priorities. It has proven impervious to criticisms regarding its work and has dismissed all calls for reform. Despite promises to improve the system made at the Seattle Ministerial Meeting in 1999, governance in the WTO has actually become worse. Rather than addressing existing inequities and power imbalances between rich and poor countries, the lobby of the rich and powerful in the WTO is attempting to expand the WTO's mandate to new areas such as environment, labour, investment, competition and government procurement.

The WTO is an entirely inappropriate institution to address issues of food and agriculture. The undersigned do not believe that the WTO will engage in profound reform in order to make itself responsive to the rights and needs of ordinary people. The WTO is attempting to establish rules to protect foreign investments of fleets that operate in national waters, and is pressuring the governments to yield exclusive fishing rights to the international consortiums. Therefore, the undersigned are calling for all food and agricultural concerns to be taken out of WTO jurisdiction through the dismantling of the Agreement on Agriculture (AoA) and removing or amending the relevant clauses on other WTO agreements so as to ensure the full exclusion of food and agriculture from the WTO regime. These include: the Agreement on Trade Related Intellectual Property Rights (TRIPs), Sanitary and Phytosanitary measures (SPS), Technical Barriers to Trade (TBT), Quantitative Restrictions (QRs), Subsidies and Countervailing Measures (SCM) and the General Agreement on Trade in Services (GATS).

A role for trade rules in agricultural and food policies?

Trade in food can play a positive role, for example, in times of regional food insecurity, or in the case of products that can only be grown in certain parts of the world, or for the exchange of quality products. However, trade rules must respect the precautionary principle in policies at all levels, recognize democratic and participatory decision making, and place peoples' food sovereignty before the imperatives of international trade.

new
int'l
framework

An alternative framework

To complement the role of local and national governments, there is a clear need for a new and alternative international framework for multilateral regulation on the sustainable production and trade of food, fish and other agricultural goods. Within this framework, the following principles must be respected:

- Peoples' food sovereignty;

- The rights of all countries to protect their domestic markets by regulating all imports that undermine their food sovereignty;

- Trade rules that support and guarantee food sovereignty;

- Upholding gender equity and equality in all policies and practices concerning food production;

- The precautionary principle;

- The right to information about the origin and content of food items;

- Genuine international democratic participation mechanisms;

- Priority to domestic food production, sustainable farming and fishing practices and equitable access to all resources;

- Support for small farmers and producers to own, and have sufficient control over means of food production;

- Support for open access of traditional fishing communities to aquatic resources;

- Effective bans on all forms of dumping, in order to protect domestic food production. This would include supply management by exporting countries to avoid surpluses and the rights of importing countries to protect internal markets against imports at low prices;

- Prohibition of biopiracy and patents on living matter – animals, plants, the human body and other life forms – and any of its components, including the development of sterile varieties through genetic engineering; and

- Respect for all human rights conventions and related multilateral agreements under independent international jurisdiction. The undersigned affirm the demands made in other civil society statements, such as Our World is Not for Sale: WTO-Shrink or Sink, and Stop the GATS Attack Now. We urge governments to immediately take the following steps: Cease negotiations to initiate a new round of trade liberalization and halt discussions to bring 'new issues' into the WTO. This includes further discussions on such issues as investment, competition, government procurement, biotechnology, services, labour and environment.

- Cancel further trade liberalization negotiations on the WTO's AoA through the WTO's built-in agenda.

- Cancel the obligation of accepting the minimum importation of 5 per cent of internal consumption; all compulsory market access clauses must similarly be cancelled immediately.

- Undertake a thorough review of both the implementation, and the environmental and social impacts of existing trade rules and agreements (and the WTO's role in this system) in relation to food, fisheries and agriculture.

- Initiate measures to remove food and agriculture from under the control of the WTO through the dismantling of the AoA and through the removal or amendment of relevant clauses in the TRIPS, GATS, SPS, TBT and SCM agreements. Replace these with a new Convention on Food Sovereignty and Trade in Food, Agriculture and Fisheries.

- Revise intellectual property policies to prohibit the patenting of living matter and any of their components and limit patent protections in order to protect public health and public safety;

- Halt all negotiations on GATS, and dismantle the principle of 'progressive liberalization' in order to protect social services and the public interest;

- Implement genuine agrarian reform and ensure the rights of peasants to crucial assets such as land, seed, water and other resources;

- Promote the primary role of fish harvesters' and fish workers' organizations in managing the use of aquatic resources and oceans, nationally and internationally.

- Initiate discussions on an alternative international framework on the sustainable production and trade of food, agricultural goods and fisheries products.

This framework should include:

- A reformed and strengthened United Nations (UN), active and committed to protecting the fundamental rights of all peoples, as being the appropriate forum to develop and negotiate rules for sustainable production and fair trade;

- An independent dispute settlement mechanism integrated within an international Court of Justice, especially to prevent dumping and GM food aid;

- A World Commission on Sustainable Agriculture and Food Sovereignty established to undertake a comprehensive assessment of the impacts of trade liberalization on food sovereignty and security, and develop proposals for change. This would include agreements and rules within the WTO and other regional and international trade regimes, and the economic policies promoted by International Financial Institutions and Multilateral Development Banks. Such a commission could be constituted of and directed by representatives from various social and cultural groups, peoples' movements, professional fields, democratically elected representatives and appropriate multi-lateral institutions;

- An international, legally binding Treaty that defines the rights of peasants and small producers to the assets, resources and legal protections they need to be able to exercise their right to produce. Such a treaty could be framed within the UN Human Rights framework, and linked to already existing relevant UN conventions;

- An International Convention that replaces the current Agreement on Agriculture (AoA) and relevant clauses from other WTO agreements and implements within the international policy framework the concept of food sovereignty and the basic human rights of all peoples to safe and healthy food, decent and full rural employment, labour rights and protection, and a healthy, rich and diverse natural environment and incorporate trading rules on food and agriculture commodities.

Creating crisis

The governments of both developed and developing countries face the choice of sacrificing the rights of the majority of their populations to food sovereignty and decent employment in return for increased corporate access to international markets. As agriculture negotiations in the World Trade Organisation (WTO) continue, government negotiators are being pressured to cede the ability of local and national governments to democratically establish their own policies to feed their people and support their farmers in return for increased access to international markets for their main exporters.

The WTO must get out of agriculture to ensure people's food sovereignty throughout the world, as the WTO is the antithesis of the idea of sovereign peoples making their own decisions about food.

Despite skirmishes among the major trading countries and

various developing country groupings on specific targets and numbers, WTO members seem unwilling to accept the fact that the fundamental problem lies in the very structure of the World Trade Organization and the framework of the Agreement on Agriculture. Through disciplines for its three 'pillars' (market access, domestic supports and export subsidies), the AoA furthers and entrenches monopoly production in the hands of the world's largest agriculture producers and exporters, while the rest of the world suffers. And as negotiations over the past ten years have shown time and again, the WTO is not a space for cooperation, but rather for competition.

Since the collapse of the WTO Ministerial Meeting in Cancún, the United States (US) and European Union (EU) have attempted to revive stalled trade talks by invoking the so-called Doha Development Agenda. However, they have not come up with any new proposals that seriously address the concerns raised by developing countries in Cancún regarding agriculture trade, such as the EU-US formula for tariff reduction, their unwillingness to actually cut export subsidies (rather than simply say they will) and their repeated attempts to hide subsidies by moving them between the Green and Blue boxes. Nor have the trade majors made any attempt to address the concerns of the thousands of farmers who gathered in Cancún to demand their rights to food sovereignty and livelihoods, thus showing complete indifference to the reasons that led Mr Lee, a Korean farmer, to sacrifice his life in protest.

What the Cancún Ministerial collapse revealed was the need and right of developing countries to protect their farmers, their agriculture and food sovereignty. Yet this is precisely what is being ignored by all WTO members in the follow-up since Cancún.

The WTO has no business in either food or agriculture. WTO rules militate against the very concept of food sovereignty. In order to protect and ensure the rights of millions of rural and urban poor in the world to food, employment and livelihoods, the WTO must be removed from food and agriculture.

Notes

1 From the album *Slash and Burn*. Listen to this song at http://www.stephansmith.com/slashandburn.html
2 See http://www.nffc.net
3 See How the WTO Rules Agriculture (p. 81) for an explanation of the colored boxes in the WTO.
4 See data at http://www.ers.usda.gov/data/costsandreturns/data/current/C-Corn.xls
5 Dumping refers to exporting products at prices that are below the cost of production, making it impossible for local producers in importing countries to compete.
6 See Food from Family Farms Act: A Proposal, p. 107.
7 Losch, 2004.
8 Han, 1999; Lee and Kim, 2003.
9 The arguments in this section are based on Lappé *et al.*, 1998; Bello *et al.*, 1999; Bello, 2001; Kwa, 2001; de Grassi and Rosset, forthcoming; Rosset, 1999a, 1999b, 2001, 2002a, 2003; Losch, 2004.
10 Rosset, 1999a; Kwa, 2001.
11 Goldschmidt, 1978.
12 Lappé *et al.*, 1998.
13 Leite *et al.*, 2004.
14 MST, 2001.
15 Rosset, 1999a.
16 Via Campesina, 2003.
17 See Government Negotiating Blocs, p. 89.
18 Bello, 2005.
19 Bello *et al.*, 1999.

20 McMichael, 2004.
21 http://www.wto.org
22 Most of this history is summarized from Wallach and Woodall, 2004; McMichael, 2004; http://www.wto.org; and http://www.citizen.org/trade
23 Gerson, 2002.
24 http://www.citizen.org/trade
25 Chase, 2003, for example.
26 Zoellick, 2003, http://www.stoptheftaa.org
27 See http://www.bilaterals.org and http://www.stoptheftaa.org
28 Bello, 2005.
29 Losch, 2004; Rosset, 1999a.
30 Losch, 2004; Rosset, 1999a.
31 http://www.viacampesina.org
32 Via Campesina *et al.*, undated; Via Campesina, 2003; Rosset, 2003; McMichael, 2004. Desmarais, 2002.
33 For example, see McMichael, 2004 and Desmarais, 2002.
34 See People's Food Sovereignty Statement, p. 125.
35 Berthelot, 2003.
36 For example, see the *New York Times* editorial titled 'The Long Reach of King Cotton' (*New York Times*, 5 August 2003).
37 Gillson *et al.*, 2004.
38 Bello, 2005; Khor, 2005.
39 Becker, 2004.
40 Becker, 2004.
41 http://www.viacampesina.org
42 Data from the Environmental Working Group at http://www.ewg.org/farm
43 Allen, 2002.
44 See http://www.oxfam.org/en/news/pressreleases/2005/ pr051212_cap
45 Eurostat, 2003 (data from 1995–2000).
46 Wise, 2005b.
47 Rosset, 2003.
48 Lilliston, 2004.
49 Wise, 2004a, 2004b.
50 Ritchie *et al.*, 2004.
51 Ritchie *et al.*, 2003, 2004.
52 Ritchie *et al.*, 2004.
53 World Bank, 2003.

54 See Wise, 2004b and Berthelot, 2004, for more details on this campaign.
55 http://www.nytimes.com/ref/opinion/harvesting-poverty.html?page
    - wanted=all
56 See Wise, 2004b; Berthelot, 2004; Wright, 2003; Weisbrot, 2004.
57 Ray *et al.*, 2003.
58 Summarized by Wise, 2004b.
59 Interview by email, 9 February 2006.
60 Ray *et al.*, 2003; Wise, 2004b; Hayenga and Wisner, 2000; Heffernan and Hendrickson, 2002; Hendrickson and Heffernan, 2002; Hendrickson *et al.*, 2001; Patel and Memarsadeghi, 2003; Murphy, 1999; Vorley, 2003; ETC Group, 2003c.
61 Compiled by Patel and Memarsadeghi, 2003.
62 IFAP, 2002; ETC Group, 2003c.
63 Krebs, 1999.
64 The material in this box is largely based on: WTO, 2004; Khor, 2003, 2004; Berthelot, 2004; Wallach and Woodall; 2004; Murphy, 2003; Green, 2003; Nadal, 2004.
65 Rosset, 2002b.
66 See http://www.ustr.gov/Who_We_Are/Bios/Richard_T_Crowder.html
67 Wise, 2005b.
68 Wise, 2004b.
69 See, for example, Lauck, 2000, and Krebs, 1991.
70 Interview by email, February 9, 2006.
71 Ray *et al.*, 2003.
72 Ritchie *et al.*, 2004.
73 Ritchie *et al.*, 2004.
74 Brusell, 2001.
75 Lappé *et al.*, 1998; Rosset, 1999b.
76 See, for example, Rodrick, 1999; Stiglitz, 2000.
77 Weisbrot and Baker, 2002; Weisbrot *et al.*, 2002.
78 Yanikkaya, 2002.
79 FAO, 2000.
80 Carlsen, 2003b.
81 Data from the World Bank's World Development Indicators at http://www.worldbank.org
82 Damian and Boltvinik, 2003.
83 De Ita, 2003.
84 Wallach and Woodall, 2004.

85 De Ita, 2003.

86 De Ita, 2003.

87 Wise, 2004b.

88 Carlsen, 2003a.

89 Ritchie *et al.*, 2003.

90 De Ita, 2003; Henriques and Patel, 2003; GRAIN, 2004.

91 Carlsen, 2003a; Barkin, 2002.

92 Carlsen, 2003a.

93 Henriques and Patel, 2003.

94 Carlsen, 2003a.

95 De Ita, 2003.

96 De Ita, 2003.

97 MINSA is a Mexican company created in 1993 from the privatization of Conasupo, the parastatal grain marketing enterprise, and is 46% owned by an American investment bank (MINSA, 2003).

98 Nadal, 2000. The rise in tortilla prices can be attributed to two factors: the removal of consumer subsidies as part of neoliberal economic reforms, and the concentration of the national tortilla commodity chain in the hands of just two companies.

99 De Ita, 2003.

100 ETC Group 2002, 2003a, 2003b.

101 Carlsen, 2003a.

102 Carlsen, 2003a.

103 Carlsen, 2003a.

104 Oyejide, 2004.

105 Berthelot, 2003.

106 IMF, 1999a, 1999b.

107 Lappé *et al*, 1998; Rosset, 1999a.

108 De Grassi and Rosset, forthcoming.

109 Almost all of the key civil society players are members of the Our World is Not for Sale Network (http://www.ourworldisnot forsale.org/), yet there is a division among them, between many of the policy-thinktank and environmentalist type of non-governmental organizations (NGOs) active on these issues, and the majority of the worlds organizations of family farmers, peasants and indigenous peoples, grouped together in the Via Campesina global alliance. Major NGO players who believe to some extent in the 'inside' strategy of fighting for better trade agreements include Third World Network, ActionAid, and Oxfam, among others. Those NGOs more closely aligned with the Via Campesina call to get trade agreements

completely out of the business of regulating food and agriculture are grouped into the Agriculture Trade Network (http://www.peoples foodsovereignty.org/), and include GRAIN, ETC Group, and Focus on the Global South.

110 Wise, 2004a, 2004b; Ritchie *et al.*, 2003; Via Campesina, 2003; CPE and NFFC, 2004.

111 Naylor, 2000.

112 Wise, 2004a, 2004b; Ritchie *et al.*, 2003; Ray *et al.*, 2003; Via Campesina, 2003; Via Campesina *et al.*, 2004.

113 Interview by email, 9 February 2006.

114 Ray *et al.*, 2003.

115 Goh, 2004.

116 Lines, 2004.

117 See the wealth of resources on-line at http://www.agribusiness accountability.org/

118 Murphy, 1999; Wise, 2004; Heffernan and Hendrickson, 2002; Hendrickson and Heffernan, 2002; Hendrickson *et al.*, 2001; Patel and Memarsadeghi, 2003.

119 BBC, 2002.

120 CPE and NFFC, 2004; Via Campesina, 2003; Via Campesina *et al.* 2004; Via Campesina *et al.*, undated.

121 GRAIN, 2004; Wallach and Woodall, 2004; see the web sites of the ETC Group (http://www.etcgroup.org) and GRAIN (http://www. grain.org) on these issues.

122 See his famous essay, 'Why reform of the WTO is the wrong agenda,' in Bello, 2001.

123 See Wallach and Woodall, 2004, for a description of how the WTO works.

124 Bello, 2002.

125 Wallach and Woodall, 2004.

126 See http://www.nffc.net/issues/fnf/fnf_13.html to learn about the proposed Food from Family Farms Act.

127 CPE, 2003.

128 Wise, 2004.

129 This box is largely based on WTO, 2004; Khor 2003, 2004; Berthelot, 2004; Wallach and Woodall, 2004; Murphy, 2003; Green, 2003; and Nadal, 2004.

130 Berthelot, 2004.

131 This box is largely based on Fontagné and Jean, 2003; Losch, 2004; Green, 2003; Raghavan, 2004; Narlikar and Tussie, 2004; G10, 2004;

Bullard, 2004; Via Campesina *et al.*, 2004; and the author's own impressions at numerous trade forums and summits.

132 CPE and NFFC, 2004.

133 Via Campesina, 2003

134 http://www.nffc.net/resources/factsheets/Food%20From%20 Family%20Farms%20Act.pdf

135 http://www.cpefarmers.org/positions/en/17_171103.pdf

136 Or the level should be discussed according to the desired relationship between the market and public support in generating farm income.

137 Downloaded from http://www.peoplesfoodsovereignty.org on 31 March 2006.

Bibliography

Allen, Mike. 2002. 'Bush Signs Bill Providing Big Farm Subsidy Increase', *Washington Post*, 14 May 2002.

Agriculture Online News. 2002. 'Veneman Outlines Ambitious WTO Proposal.' Wire service report, 26 July 2002. http://www.agriculture.com/default.sph/AgNews.class?FNC=side BarMore__ANewsin

Barkin, David. 2002. 'The Reconstruction of a Modern Mexican Peasantry', *Journal of Peasant Studies* 30 (1): 73–90.

BBC. 2000. 'Trustbusters: A History Lesson', British Broadcasting Service, http://news.bbc.co.uk/1/hi/in_depth/business/2000/microsoft/63 5257.stm

Becker, Elizabeth. 2004. 'WTO rules against US on cotton subsidies', *New York Times*, 27 April 2004.

Bello, Walden. 2001. *The Future in the Balance: Essays on Globalization and Resistance*, Oakland: Food First Books.

Bello, Walden. 2002. *Deglobalization: Ideas for a New World Economy*, London: Zed Books.

Bello, Walden. 2005. 'The Real Meaning of Hong Kong: Brazil and India Join the Big Boys' Club'. Bangkok: Focus on the Global South. http://www.focusweb.org/content/view/799/36/

Bello, Walden, Shea Cunningham and Bill Rau. 1999. *Dark Victory: The United States and Global Poverty*, second edition, London and Oakland: Pluto and Food First Books.

Berthelot, Jacques. 2003. 'Cancún: Subsidies for Agribusiness', *Le Monde Diplomatique*, September.

Berthelot, Jacques. 2004. 'Ending Food Dumping: Taking the US and EU through the WTO Disputes Procedure after the Expiry of the "peace clause." ' Preliminary draft of chapters 1 to 5 of an on-going work. See http://solidarite.asso.fr/actions/Agriculture.htm

Brusell, Juli. 2001. 'Our Family Farms: a Final Requiem or a Route to Recovery?' Chicago: Conscious Choice, May 2001. http://www.consciouschoice.com/2001/cc1405/ourfamilyfarms140 5.html

Carlsen, Laura. 2003a. 'The Mexican Farmers' Movement: Exposing the Myths of Free Trade'. Interhemispheric Resource Center, http://www.americas policy.org

Carlsen, Laura. 2003b. 'The Mexican Experience and Lessons for WTO Negotiations on the Agreement on Agriculture'. Interhemispheric Resource Center, http://www.americaspolicy.org

Chase, Steven. 2003. ' "FTAA lite" Seen as Deal-Breaker'. *Toronto Globe and Mail*, 19 November 2003.

CPE. 2003. 'For a Legitimate, Sustainable and Supportive Common Agricultural Policy'. European Farmers Coordination (CPE), http://www.cpefarmers.org/ positions/en/17_171103.pdf

CPE and NFFC. 2004. 'WTO Agricultural Negotiations in Geneva. A joint statement by the European Farmers Coordination (CPE) and the National Family Farm Coalition, USA (NFFC)'. http://www.nffc.net

Damian, Araceli and Julio Boltvinik. 2003. 'Evolución y características de la pobreza en México'. *Comercio Exterior* 53(6): 519–23.

de Grassi, Aaron and Peter Rosset. Forthcoming. *A New Green Revolution for Africa? Myths and Realities of Agriculture, Technology and Development.* Oakland: Food First Books.

Desmarais, Annette. 2002. 'The Via Campesina: Consolidating an International Peasant and Farm Movement'. *Journal of Peasant Studies* 29 (2): 91–124.

de Ita, Ana. 2003. 'Diez años de TLCAN, impactos del capítulo agrícola del Tratado de Libre Comercio de América del Norte en la economía campesina y la soberanía alimentaria. Reporte para UNORCA, marzo de 2003'. Mexico City: CECCAM.

ETC Group. 2002. 'Genetic pollution in Mexico's center of maize diversity'. Institute for Food and Development Policy (Food First), *Backgrounder* 8 (2): 1–4. http://www.foodfirst.org/pubs/backgrdrs/ 2002/sp02v8n2.html

ETC Group. 2003a. 'Maize Rage in Mexico: GM Maize Contamination in Mexico – 2 years later'. *Genotype*, 10 October 2003. http://www.etcgroup.org/ article.asp?newsid=409

ETC Group. 2003b. 'Nine Mexican states found to be GM contaminated'. *News*, 11 October 2003.
http://www.etcgroup.org/article.asp?newsid=410

ETC Group. 2003c. 'Oligopoly, Inc.: Concentration in Corporate Power, 2003'. ETC Group, http://www.etcgroup.org/article.asp?newsid=420

EUROSTAT. 2003. *Eurostat Yearbook 2003*. Luxembourg: Eurostat.

FAO. 2000. FAO Symposium on Agriculture, Trade and Food Security: Issues and Options in the Forthcoming WTO Negotiations from the Perspective of Developing Countries. Geneva, 23–24 September 1999. SESSION II b: Experience with the implementation of the Uruguay Round Agreement on Agriculture – developing country experiences (based on case studies) 'Paper No. 3 Synthesis of country case studies.' Rome: Food and Agriculture Organization of the United Nations.
http://www.wtowatch.org/library/admin/uploadedfiles/Agriculture_Trade_and_Food_Security_Issues_and.pdf

FAO. 2003. *Agricultural Commodities: Profiles and Relevant WTO Negotiating Issues*. Rome: Food and Agriculture Organization of the United Nations.

Fontagné, Lionel and Sébasten Jean. 2003. 'The WTO: In the Trough of the Trade Round'. *La Lettre du CEPII* (France) 226: 1–4.
http://www.cepii.fr

Gerson, Timi. 2002. 'What happened in Quito: The Nitty Gritty'. http://www.peoplesconsultation.org/newsletter/nov2002.html

Gillson, Ian, Colin Poulton, Kelvin Balcombe and Sheila Page. 2004. 'Understanding the Impact of Cotton Subsidies on Developing Countries and Poor People in those Countries'. Draft Report. Overseas Development Institute, International Economic Development Unit, www.odi.org.uk/iedg/ cotton_report.pdf

Goh, Chien Yen. 2004. *UNCTAD XI: Calls to Break the 'Conspiracy of Silence' on Commodities*. Third World Network, TWN Report, 15 June 2004.

Goldschmidt, Walter. 1978. *As You Sow: Three Studies in the Social Consequences of Agribusiness*. New York: Allenheld, Osmun.

GRAIN. 2004. 'The disease of the day: Acute treatyitis. The Myths and Consequences of free trade agreements with the US. GRAIN, http://www.grain.org/ briefings/?id=183

Green, Duncan. 2003. 'The Cancún WTO ministerial meeting: A view from the sidelines'. *Trade Hot Topics Commonwealth* 30: 1–12.

Han, Jungsoo. 1999. 'Korea rice liberalization. Trade & Environment Database (TED)', American University, TED Case Studies, Vol. 9, No. 1, Case Study no. 513. http://www.american.edu/TED/korrice.htm

Hayenga, M. and R. Wisner. 2000. 'Cargill's Acquisition of Continental Grain's Grain Merchandising Business.' *Review of Agricultural Economics* 22 (1): 252–66.

Heffernan, W. and Mary Hendrickson. 2002. 'Multi-national Concentrated Food Processing and Marketing Systems and the Farm Crisis'. Annual Meeting of the American Association for the Advancement of Science, The Farm Crisis: How the Heck Did We Get Here?, Boston.

Hendrickson, M., W. D. Heffernan, et al. 2001. *Consolidation in Food Retailing and Dairy: Implications for Farmers and Consumers in a Global Food System*. Columbia, MO: Department of Rural Sociology, University of Missouri.

Hendrickson, M. and W. Heffernan. 2002. *Concentration of Agricultural Markets*. Columbia, MO: Department of Rural Sociology, University of Missouri.

Henriques, Gisele and Raj Patel. 2003. *Agricultural Trade Liberalization and Mexico*. Institute for Food and Development Policy (Food First), Policy Brief No. 7.

IFAP. 2002. 'Sixth Draft Report on Industrial Concentration in the Agri-Food Sector'. Paris: International Federation of Agricultural Producers.

IMF. 1999a. 'IMF Concessional Financing Though ESAF'. Factsheet, Washington, DC: IMF. http://www.imf.org/external/np/exr/facts/esaf.htm

IMF. 1999b. 'Status Report on Follow-Up to the Review of the Enhanced Structural Adjustment Facility', Policy Development and Review Department Report, Washington, DC: IMF.

Khor, Martin. 2003. *The WTO Agriculture Agreement: Features, Effects, Negotiations, and Suggested Changes*. Penang: Third World Network.

Khor, Martin 2004. *Preliminary Comments of the WTO's Geneva July Decision*. Penang: Third World Network.

Khor, Martin 2005. 'WTO Ministerial Outcome Imbalanced Against Developing Countries'. *Third World Network Info Service on WTO and Trade Issues*, 22 December 2005.

Krebs, A. V. 1991. *The Corporate Reapers: The Book of Agribusiness*. Washington, DC: Essential Books.

Krebs, A.V. 1999. 'Urgent appeal: effort to block Cargill/Continental sale public comment deadline at hand'. *Agribusiness Examiner*, No. 50, 8

October. http://www.electricarrow.com/CARP/agbiz/agex-50.html

Kwa, Aileen. 2001. 'Agriculture in Developing Countries: Which Way Forward? Small Farmers and the Need for Alternative, Development-Friendly Food Production Systems'. South Centre Occasional Papers on Trade-Related Agenda, Development and Equity (TRADE) No. 4, 22 pp., http://www.southcentre.org/publications/occasional/paper04/toc.htm#TopOfPage

Lappé, F.M., J. Collins, P. Rosset, and L. Esparza. 1998. *World Hunger: Twelve Myths*, second edition. New York: Grove Press.

Lauck, Jon. 2000. *American Agriculture and the Problem of Monopoly: The Political Economy of Grain Belt Farming, 1953–1980*. Lincoln: University of Nebraska Press.

Lee, Yong-Kee and Hanho Kim. 2003. 'Korean Agriculture after the Uruguay Round and World Agricultural Policy Reform'. Paper presented at the International Conference on Agricultural Policy Reform and the WTO: Where are we Heading? Capri (Italy), 23–26 June. http://www.ecostat.unical.it/2003agtradeconf/Contributed%20papers/Lee%20and%20Kim.pdf

Leite, Sérgio, Beatriz Heredia, Leonilde Medeiros, Moacir Palmeira, and Rosângela Cintrão. 2004. *Impactos dos Assentamentos: Um Estudo sobre o Meio Rural Brasileiro*. Brasília: Núcleo de Estudos Agrários e Desenvolvimento Rural (NEAD).

Lilliston, Ben. 2004 'WTO Ruling Against US Cotton Has Broad Ramifications for Farm Policy: Ruling Should Prompt Shift in US Programs to Lift Prices.' Press release from the Institute for Agriculture and Trade Policy, 27 April 2004, Minneapolis, MN.

Lines, Tom. 2004. 'Commodities Trade, Poverty Alleviation & Sustainable Development'. Paper presented at the Common Fund for Commodities session of UNCTAD XI in Sao Paulo, 15 June 2004. Amsterdam: Common Fund for Commodities.

Losch, Bruno. 2004. 'Debating the Multifunctionality of Agriculture: From Trade Negotiations to Development Policies by the South'. *Journal of Agrarian Change* 4 (3): 336–60.

McMichael, Philip. 2004. 'Global Development and the Corporate Food Regime'. Paper Presented at the Symposium on New Directions in the Sociology of Global Development, XI World Congress of Rural Sociology, Trondheim, Norway, July 2004.

MINSA. 2003. *Annual Report for the year ended December 31, 2002*. Tlalnepantla, Mexico. http://www.minsa.com

MST (Movimento dos Trabalhadores Rurais Sem Terra). 2001 (manuscript). *Os Empreendimentos Sociais do MST*. Sao Paolo: MST.

Murphy, Sophia. 1999. 'Market Power in Agricultural Markets: Some Issues for Developing Countries'. Working Paper, TRADE, South Centre, http://www.southcentre.org/publications/agric/toc.htm# TopOfPage

Murphy, Sophia. 2003. 'World Trade Organization Agreement on Agriculture Basics'. Cancún Series Paper no. 2. Minneapolis: Institute for Agriculture and Trade Policy.

Nadal, Alejandro. 2000. *The Environmental Impacts of Economic Liberalization on Corn Production in Mexico*. London: Oxfam and WWF International.

Nadal, Alejandro. 2004. 'Ser vago en la OMC'. *La Jornada* (Mexico), 4 August 2004.

Narlikar, Amrita, and Diana Tussie. 2004. 'Bargaining Together in Cancún: Developing Countries and their Evolving Coalitions'. Manuscript, Department of Politics, University of Exeter, UK.

Naylor, George. 2000. 'Help Family Farms, not Factory Farms'. *The Des Moines Register*, 11A, 13 January 2000.

Oyejide, T. Ademola. 2004. 'African Trade Policy in the Context of National Development Strategies'. Paper prepared for presentation at ECA's Conference of African Ministers of Finance, Planning and Economic Development holding in Kampala, 22 May 2004. http://www.uneca.org/cfm/2004/052204_African_trade_policy. htm

Patel, Raj, and Sanaz Memarsadeghi. 2003. 'Agricultural Restructuring and Concentration in the United States: Who Wins? Who Loses?' Institute for Food and Development Policy (Food First), Policy Brief No. 6.

Raghavan, Chakrvarthi. 2004. 'WTO Agriculture Meeting Postponed'. *South-North Development Monitor* (SUNS list serve), 12 July 2004.

Ray, Daryll E., Daniel G. de la Torre and Kelly J. Tiller. 2003. *Rethinking US Agricultural Policy: Changing Course to Secure Farmer Livelihoods Worldwide*. Knoxville, TN: Agricultural Policy Analysis Center, University of Tenessee. http://www.agpolicy.org/ blueprint.html

Ritchie, Mark, Sophia Murphy and Mary Beth Lake. 2003. 'United States Dumping on World Agricultural Markets'. Cancún Series Paper no. 1. Minneapolis: Institute for Agriculture and Trade Policy.

Ritchie, Mark, Sophia Murphy and Mary Beth Lake. 2004. 'United States Dumping on World Agricultural Markets. February 2004 Update'. Cancun Series Paper no. 1. Minneapolis: Institute for Agriculture and Trade Policy.

Rodrick, Dani, 1999. *The New Global Economy and Developing Countries: Making Openness Work*, Overseas Development Council.

Rosset, Peter M. 1999a. *The Multiple Functions and Benefits of Small Farm Agriculture, in the Context of Global Trade Negotiations*. Institute for Food and Development Policy (Food First), Policy Brief no. 4. http://www.foodfirst.org/pubs/policybs/pb4.html

Rosset, Peter M. 1999b. *Food First Trade Principles*. Institute for Food and Development Policy, Food First Backgrounder 5 (2): 1–4. http://www.foodfirst.org/pubs/backgrdrs/1999/f99v5n2.html

Rosset, P. 2000. 'The Potential of Small Farm Agriculture to Meet Future Food Needs'. *Proceedings of the Study Week on Food Needs of the Developing World in the Early Twenty-First Century, 27–30 January 1999*, Pontificia Academy of Sciences, Vatican City, The Vatican.

Rosset, P. 2001. *Tides Shift on Agrarian Reform: New Movements Show the Way*. Institute for Food and Development Policy, Food First Backgrounder 7 (1): 1–8. http://www.foodfirst.org/pubs/backgrdrs/2001/w01v7n1.html

Rosset, Peter M. 2002a. 'Access to Land: Land Reform and Security of Tenure'. Background Paper for the World Food Summit Plus Five, 10–13 June 2002, Rome. Rome: Food and Agriculture Organization (FAO) of the United Nations. http://www.landaction.org/display.php?article=179

Rosset, Peter. 2002b. 'The Revolving Door: Industry and the US Government in Agricultural Trade Negotiations'. Institute for Food and Development Policy (Food First), http://www.foodfirst.org/media/display.php?id=215

Rosset, Peter. 2003. 'Food Sovereignty: Global Rallying Cry of Farmer Movements'. Institute for Food and Development Policy, Food First Backgrounder 9 (4): 1–4. http://www.foodfirst.org/pubs/backgrdrs/2003/f03v9n4.html

Stam, J. M. and B. L. Dixon. 2004. *Farmer Bankruptcies and Farm Exits in the United States, 1899–2002*. USDA-ERS Agriculture Information Bulletin No. 788.

Stiglitz, Joseph. 2000. 'The Insider: What I Learned at the World Economic Crisis'. *The Daily Telegraph* (London), 9 June.

UNCTAD. 2004. *The Least Developed Countries Report 2004*. New York and Geneva: United Nations Conference On Trade And Development.

USTR. 2004. *Trade Facts*, 4 August. Office of the United States Trade Representative, http://www.ustr.gov

Via Campesina. 2003. 'It is Urgent to Re-orient the Debate on Agriculture and Initiate a Policy of Food Sovereignty'. Via Campesina, http://www.viacampesina.org/art_english.php3?id_article=275

Via Campesina *et al.* 2004. 'Statement on Agriculture after Cancún: Peasants, Family Farmers, Fisherfolk and their Supporters Propose People's Food Sovereignty as alternative to US/EU and G20 positions'. Via Campesina and other signatories, http://www. viacampesina.org/art_english.php3?id_article=286

Via Campesina *et al.* Undated. 'People's Food Sovereignty Food and Agriculture Statement'. http://www.peoplesfoodsovereignty.org/ statements/new%20statement/statement_01.htm

Vorley, B. 2003. *Food, Inc.: Corporate Concentration from Farmer to Consumer.* London, UK Food Group.

Wade, R. H. 2004. 'Is Globalization Reducing Poverty and Inequality?' *World Development* 32 (4): 567–89.

Wallach, Lori and Patrick Woodall. 2004. *Whose Trade Organization? A Comprehensive Guide to the WTO.* New York: New Press and Public Citizen.

Weisbrot, Mark. 2004. 'No Boost for Development in World Trade Negotiations'. Center for Economic and Policy Research (CEPR), http://www.cepr.net/columns/weisbrot/wto_geneva_8_03_04.htm

Weisbrot, Mark and Dean Baker. 2002. 'The Relative Impact of Trade Liberalization on Developing Countries'. Center for Economic and Policy Research, http://www.cepr.net/relative_impact_of_trade_ liberal.htm

Weisbrot, Mark, Dean Baker, Robert Naiman and Gila Neta. 2002. 'Growth May Be Good for the Poor – But are IMF and World Bank Policies Good for Growth? A Closer Look at the World Bank's Most Recent Defense of Its Policies'. Center for Economic and Policy Research, http://www.cepr.net/ response_to_dollar_kraay.htm

Wise, Timothy A. 2004a. 'Barking up the Wrong Tree: Agricultural Subsidies, Dumping and Policy Reform'. *Bridges* 5: 3–5.

Wise, Timothy A. 2004b. 'The Paradox of Agricultural Subsidies: Measurement Issues, Agricultural Dumping, and Policy Reform'. Global Development and Environment Institute, Tufts University, Working Paper No. 04-02.

Wise, Timothy A. 2005a. 'Understanding the Farm Problem: Six Common Errors in Presenting Farm Statistics'. Global Development and Environment Institute, Tufts University, Working Paper No. 05-02.

Wise, Timothy A. 2005b. 'Identifying the Real Winners from US

Agricultural Policies'. Global Development and Environment Institute, Tufts University, Working Paper No. 05-07.

World Bank. 2003. *Global Economic Prospects 2004: Realizing the Development Promise of the Doha Agenda*. Washington: World Bank.

Wright, Joseph. 2003.' The \$300 Billion Question: How Much Do the Governments of High-income Countries Subsidize Agriculture?' Center for Economic Policy Research (CEPR), http://www.cepr.net

WTO. 2004. 'Agriculture Negotiations: Backgrounder'. Updated 20 April 2004. http://www.wto.org/english/tratop_e/agric_e/negs_bkgrnd 05_intro_e.htm

Yanikkaya, Halit. 2002. 'Trade Openness and Economic Growth: A Cross-country Empirical Investigation'. *Journal of Development Economics* 72 (2003) 57– 89.

Zoellick, Robert B. 2003. 'America will not Wait for the Won't Do Countries.' *Financial Times*, 22 September 2003.

Index

About this series

'Communities in the South are facing great difficulties in coping with global trends. I hope this brave new series will throw much needed light on the issues ahead and help us choose the right options.'
MARTIN KHOR, *Director,*
Third World Network, Penang

'There is no more important campaign than our struggle to bring the global economy under democratic control. But the issues are fearsomely complex. This Global Issues series is a valuable resource for the committed campaigner and the educated citizen.'
BARRY COATES, *Director,*
World Development Movement (WDM)

'Zed Books has long provided an inspiring list about the issues that touch and change people's lives. The Global Issues series is another dimension of Zed's fine record, allowing access to a range of subjects and authors that, to my knowledge, very few publishers have tried. I strongly recommend these new, powerful titles and this exciting series.'
JOHN PILGER, *author*

'We are all part of a generation that actually has the means to eliminate extreme poverty world-wide. Our task is to harness the forces of globalization for the benefit of working people, their families and their communities – that is our collective duty. The Global Issues series makes a powerful contribution to the global campaign for justice, sustainable and equitable development, and peaceful progress.'
GLENYS KINNOCK, *MEP*

The Global Issues series

ALREADY AVAILABLE

- Peggy Antrobus, *The Global Women's Movement: Origins, Issues and Strategies*
- Walden Bello, *Deglobalization: Ideas for a New World Economy*
- Robert Ali Brac de la Perrière and Franck Seuret, *Brave New Seeds: The Threat of GM Crops to Farmers*
- Greg Buckman, *Globalization: Tame It or Scrap It?*
- Greg Buckman, *Global Trade: Past Mistakes, Future Choices*
- Ha-Joon Chang and Ilene Grabel, *Reclaiming Development: An Alternative Economic Policy Manual*
- Koen De Feyter, *Human Rights: Social Justice in the Age of the Market*
- Oswaldo de Rivero, *The Myth of Development: The Non-viable Economies of the 21st Century*
- Graham Dunkley, *Free Trade: Myth, Reality and Alternatives*
- Joyeeta Gupta, *Our Simmering Planet: What to do about Global Warming?*
- Nicholas Guyatt, *Another American Century? The United States and the World since 9.11*
- Ann-Christin Sjölander Holland, *Water for Sale? Corporations against People*
- Martin Khor, *Rethinking Globalization: Critical Issues and Policy Choices*
- John Madeley, *Food for All: The Need for a New Agriculture*
- John Madeley, *Hungry for Trade: How the Poor Pay for Free Trade*
- Damien Millet and Eric Toussaint, *Who Owes Who? 50 Questions About World Debt*
- Paola Monzini, *Sex Traffic: Prostitution, Crime, and Exploitation*
- Jonathon W. Moses, *International Migration: Globalization's Last Frontier*
- A. G. Noorani, *Islam and Jihad: Prejudice versus Reality*
- Riccardo Petrella, *The Water Manifesto: Arguments for a World Water Contract*
- Peter Robbins, *Stolen Fruit: The Tropical Commodities Disaster*
- Peter M. Rosset, *Food is Different: Why We Must Get the WTO Out of Agriculture*
- Toby Shelley, *Oil: Politics, Poverty and the Planet*
- Toby Shelley, *Nanotechnology: New Promises, New Dangers*
- Vandana Shiva, *Protect or Plunder? Understanding Intellectual Property Rights*
- Harry Shutt, *A New Democracy: Alternatives to a Bankrupt World Order*
- David Sogge, *Give and Take: What's the Matter with Foreign Aid?*
- Vivien Stern, *Creating Criminals: Prisons and People in a Market Society*
- Paul Todd and Jonathan Bloch, *Global Intelligence: The World's Secret Services Today*

IN PREPARATION

Liz Kelly, *Violence against Women*
Alan Marshall, *A New Nuclear Age? The Case for Nuclear Power Revisited*
Roger Moody, *Digging the Dirt: The Modern World of Global Mining*
Edgar Pieterse, *City Futures: Confronting the Crisis of Urban Development*

For full details of this list and Zed's other subject and general catalogues, please write to: The Marketing Department, Zed Books, 7 Cynthia Street, London N1 9JF, UK or email Sales@zedbooks.net

Visit our website at: www.zedbooks.co.uk

Participating organizations

Both ENDS A service and advocacy organization which collaborates with environment and indigenous organizations, both in the South and in the North, with the aim of helping to create and sustain a vigilant and effective environmental movement.

Nieuwe Keizersgracht 45, 1018 vc Amsterdam, The Netherlands
Phone: +31 20 623 0823 • Fax: +31 20 620 8049
Email: info@bothends.org • Website: www.bothends.org

Catholic Institute for International Relations (CIIR) CIIR aims to contribute to the eradication of poverty through a programme that combines advocacy at national and international level with community-based development.

Unit 3, Canonbury Yard, 190a New North Road, London N1 7BJ, UK
Phone: +44 (0)20 7354 0883 • Fax +44 (0)20 7359 0017
Email: ciir@ciir.org • Website: www.ciir.org

Corner House The Corner House is a UK-based research and solidarity group working on social and environmental justice issues in North and South.

PO Box 3137, Station Road, Sturminster Newton, Dorset DT10 1YJ, UK
Tel.: +44 (0)1258 473795 • Fax: +44 (0)1258 473748
Email: cornerhouse@gn.apc.org • Website: www.cornerhouse.icaap.org

Council on International and Public Affairs (CIPA) CIPA is a human rights research, education and advocacy group, with a particular focus on economic and social rights in the USA and elsewhere around the world. Emphasis in recent years has been given to resistance to corporate domination.

777 United Nations Plaza, Suite 3C, NewYork, NY 10017, USA
Tel.: +1 212 972 9877 • Fax +1 212 972 9878
Email: cipany@igc.org • Website: www.cipa-apex.org

Dag Hammarskjöld Foundation The Dag Hammarskjöld Foundation, established in 1962, organizes seminars and workshops on social, economic and cultural issues facing developing countries with a particular focus on alternative and innovative solutions. Results are published in its journal *Development Dialogue*.

Övre Slottsgatan 2, 753 10 Uppsala, Sweden.
Tel.: +46 18 102772 • Fax: +46 18 122072
Email: secretariat@dhf.uu.se • Website: www.dhf.uu.se

Development GAP The Development Group for Alternative Policies is a Non-Profit Development Resource Organization working with popular organizations in the South and their Northern partners in support of a development that is truly sustainable and that advances social justice.

927 15th Street NW, 4th Floor, Washington, DC, 20005, USA
Tel.: +1 202 898 1566 • Fax: +1 202 898 1612
Email: dgap@igc.org • Website: www.developmentgap.org

Focus on the Global South Focus is dedicated to regional and global policy analysis and advocacy work. It works to strengthen the capacity of organizations of the poor and marginalized people of the South and to better analyse and understand the impacts of the globalization process on their daily lives.

C/o CUSPLI, Chulalongkorn University, Bangkok 10330, Thailand
Tel.: +66 2 218 7363 • Fax: +66 2 255 9976
Email: Admin@focusweb.org • Website: www.focusweb.org

IBON   IBON Foundation is a research, education and information institution that provides publications and services on socio-economic issues as support to advocacy in the Philippines and abroad. Through its research and databank, formal and non-formal education programmes, media work and international networking, IBON aims to build the capacity of both Philippine and international organizations.

Room 303 SCC Bldg, 4427 Int. Old Sta. Mesa, Manila 1008, Philippines
Phone: +632 7132729 • Fax +632 716108
Email: editors@ibon.org • Website: www.ibon.org

Inter Pares   Inter Pares, a Canadian social justice organization, has been active since 1975 in building relationships with Third World development groups and providing support for community-based development programmes. Inter Pares is also involved in education and advocacy in Canada, promoting understanding about the causes, effects and solutions to poverty.

221 Laurier Avenue East, Ottawa, Ontario, KIN 6PI Canada
Phone: +1 613 563 4801 • Fax +1 613 594 4704
Email: info@interpares.ca • Website: www.interpares.ca

Public Interest Research Centre   PIRC is a research and campaigning group based in Delhi which seeks to serve the information needs of activists and organizations working on macro-economic issues concerning finance, trade and development.

142 Maitri Apartments, Plot No. 28, Patparganj, Delhi 110092, India Phone: +91 11 22210SI/2432054 • Fax: +91 11 2224233
Email: kaval@nde.vsnl.net.in

Third World Network   TWN is an international network of groups and individuals involved in efforts to bring about a greater articulation of the needs and rights of peoples in the Third World; a fair distribution of the world's resources; and forms of development which are ecologically sustainable and fulfil human needs. Its international secretariat is based in Penang, Malaysia.

121-S Jalan Utama, 10450 Penang, Malaysia
Tel.: +60 4 226 6159 • Fax: +60 4 226 4505
Email: twnet@po.jaring.my • Website: www.twnside.org.sg

Third World Network–Africa   TWN–Africa is engaged in research and advocacy on economic, environmental and gender issues. In relation to its current particular interest in globalization and Africa, its work focuses on trade and investment, the extractive sectors and gender and economic reform.

2 Ollenu Street, East Legon, PO Box AN19452, Accra-North, Ghana. Tel.: +233 21 511189/503669/500419 • Fax: +233 21 511188
Email: twnafrica@ghana.com

World Development Movement (WDM)   The World Development Movement campaigns to tackle the causes of poverty and injustice. It is a democratic membership movement that works with partners in the South to cancel unpayable debt and break the ties of IMF conditionality, for fairer trade and investment rules, and for strong international rules on multinationals.

25 Beehive Place, London SW9 7QR, UK
Tel.: +44 (0)20 7737 6215 • Fax: +44 (0)20 7274 8232
Email: wdm@wdm.org.uk • Website: www.wdm.org.uk

This book is also available in the following countries

CARIBBEAN
Arawak Publications
17 Kensington Crescent,
Apt 5,
Kingston 5
Jamaica
Tel: 876 960 7538
Fax: 876 960 9219

EGYPT
MERIC (The Middle East
Readers' Information Center)
2 Bahgat Ali Street,
Tower D/Apt. 24
Zamalek
Cairo
Tel: 20 2 735 3818/736 3824
Fax: 20 2 736 9355

FIJI
University Book Centre
University of South Pacific,
Suva
Tel: 679 313 900
Fax: 679 303 265

GUYANA
Austin's Book Services
190 Church Street
Cummingsburg
Georgetown
Tel: 592 227 7395
Fax: 592 227 7396
Email: Austins@guyana.net.gy

IRAN
Book City
743 North Hafez Avenue
15977 Tehran
Tel: 98 21 889 7875
Fax: 98 21 889 7785
Email: Bookcity@neda.net

MAURITIUS
Editions Le Printemps
4 Club Road
Vacoas
Mauritius

NAMIBIA
Book Den
PO Box 3469
Shop 4, Frans Indongo
Gardens
Windhoek
Tel: 264 61 239976
Fax: 264 61 234248

NEPAL
Everest Media Services
GPO Box 5443, Dillibazar
Putalisadak Chowk
Kathmandu
Tel: 977 1 416026
Fax: 977 1 250176

NIGERIA
Mosuro Publishers
52 Magazine Road
Jericho, Ibadan
Nigeria
Tel: 234 2 241 3375
Fax: 234 2 241 3374

PAKISTAN
Vanguard Books
45 The Mall
Lahore
Tel: 92 42 735 5079
Fax: 92 42 735 5197

PAPUA NEW GUINEA
Unisearch PNG Pty Ltd
Box 320, University
National Capital District
Tel: 675 326 0130
Fax: 675 326 0127

RWANDA
Librairie Ikirezi
PO Box 443,
Kigali
Tel/Fax: 250 71314

SUDAN
The Nile Bookshop
New Extension Street 41
P O Box 8036
Khartoum
Tel: 249 11 463 749

UGANDA
Aristoc Booklex Ltd
PO Box 5130, Kampala
Road
Diamond Trust Building
Kampala
Tel/Fax: 256 41 254867

ZAMBIA
UNZA Press
PO Box 32379
Lusaka
Tel: 260 1 290409
Fax: 260 1 253952

Acknowledgment of Sources

The publishers gratefully acknowledge permission to reproduce the following material. Any omissions are entirely unintentional, and the publishers would be glad, if notified, to make due acknowledgment in future editions.

The lyrics of the song 'Lee Kyung Hae' from the album *Slash and Burn*, Universal Hobo/Artemis Records, 2004 © 2004 Stephan Smith Publishing, ASCAP

Figure 3 (Mexico: Real Maize Subsidies, 1994–2002), from 'The Paradox of Agricultural Subsidies: Measurement Issues, Agricultural Dumping, and Policy Reform', Global Development and Environment Institute Working Paper no. 04-02 © Global Development and Environment Institute, 2004

Graph 5 (Corn Imports and US Subsidies), from *Policy Brief No. 7: Agricultural Trade Liberalization and Mexico* by Gisele Henriques and Raj Patel © Institute of Food and Development Policy/Food First, 2003

Graph (Index of World Market Price for Meat), from *Agricultural Commodities: Profiles and Relevant WTO Negotiating Issues*, published by Food and Agriculture Organization of the United Nations © Food and Agriculture Organization of the United Nations, 2003

Graph (Global Price Trends for Wheat and Maize, Corrected for Inflation), from *Agricultural Commodities: Profiles and Relevant WTO Negotiating Issues*, published by Food and Agriculture Organization of the United Nations © Food and Agriculture Organization of the United Nations, 2003

Printed in the United States
76366LV00003BA/157-498